Chinese Archaeological Discoveries

The Legend of
Mawangdui

Edited by Zhang Dongxia

China Intercontinental Press

01

02

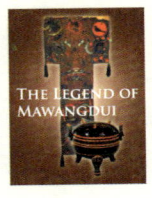
03

04

05

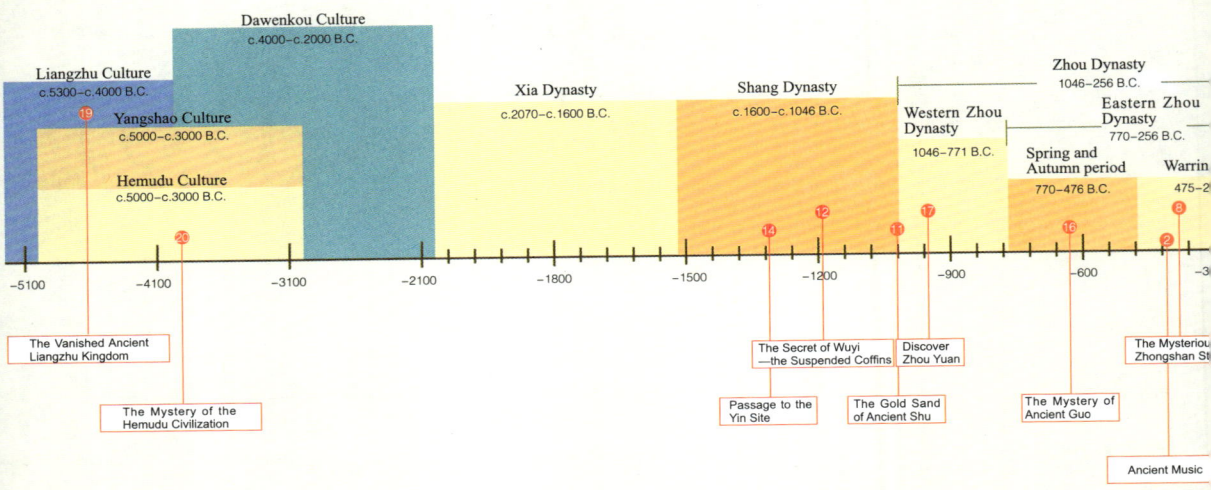

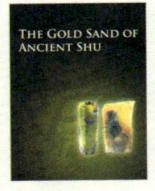
11

12

13

14

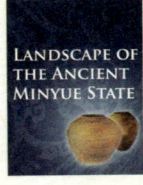
15

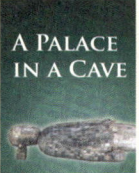

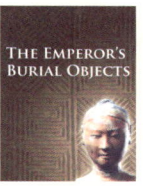

06　　　　07　　　　08　　　　09　　　　10

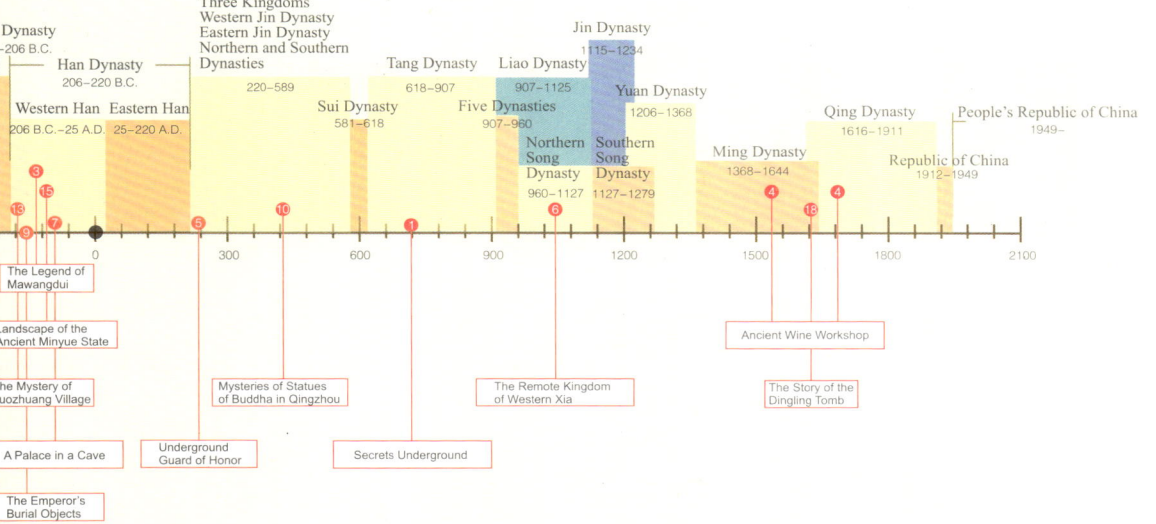

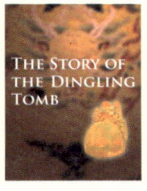

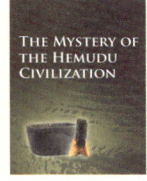

16　　　　17　　　　18　　　　19　　　　20

CONTENTS

   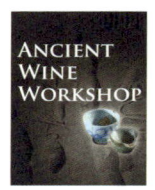 

Secrets Underground......6

Ancient Music......28

The Legend of Mawangdui......50

Ancient Wine Workshop......84

Underground Guard of Honor......106

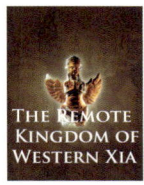 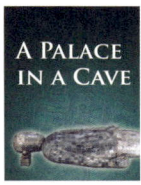 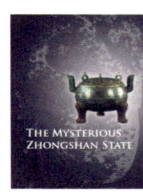  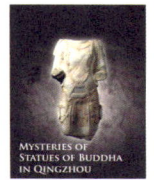

The Remote Kingdom of Western Xia......126

A Palace in a Cave......148

The Mysterious Zhongshan State......174

The Emperor's Burial Objects......194

Mysteries of Statues of Buddha in Qingzhou......218

Secrets Underground

In the fall of 1981, a rampant rainstorm ravaged the Guanzhong plain of Shanxi province. A pagoda was hit and halved by the bolt. Buddhist scriptures and statues of Buddha fell into ruin. The monks were dumbfounded by the sudden strike of the storm. Nobody then could ever imagine that the collapse of the pagoda would unveil a secret hidden underground for thousands of years.

SECRETS
UNDERGROUND

Xi'an, of northwestern China, used to be the capital of 11 dynasties in Chinese history. Around its suburban region, there are numerous imperial tombs and palaces of ancient times, including the world-renowned terracotta army.

Famen temple is another famous ancient site. It is located in Fufeng County, 110 km away from Xi'an. The earliest description of this Buddhist temple was in the Northern Wei dynasty from around the 5th century. But according to local folklore, its existence stretches back to the early stages of Buddhism's introduction to China.

Buddhism originated in ancient India. Its founder, Sakyamuni, was a prince of an Indian tribe. He gave up his life of luxury at the age of 29 and founded the Buddhist religion after realizing the true meaning of life under a bodhi tree. In 486 AD, Sakyamuni died in a forest in Northern India at the age of 80. His body was cremated and the crystal remains, known as Sariras, were preserved as sacred Buddhist articles.

250 years after Sakyamuni's death, the great Indian king, King Asoka, unified warring India and converted to Buddhism

The Terracotta Warriors in Qin Shihuang's Imperial Mausoleum

in his late years. To promote and spread Buddhism, he gathered up the Sariras and distributed them to various regions around the world. As the story goes, some of the Sariras were carried to China. As a result, Buddhist pagodas emerged all over China to enshrine the sacred Sariras. Famen Temple was one of them.

Han Jinke

Head of Fufeng Cultural Bureau and one of the participants of the excavation. He was the first to discover the secret underneath the pagoda.

It was February 27th 1987 when we started the excavation with this foundation and were digging a cross-shaped whole. On April 2nd, our shovel bounced back against a stone surface. Clearing off the dirt, there appeared a marble cover about 1 square meter across. Northwest to the cover were three pieces of gravel.

In Buddhism, a pagoda is built to contain Sarira. In India, pagodas are shaped like tombs while the ones in China inherit the Chinese architectural tradition. It has been said that the Famen pagoda in the Tang dynasty was constructed from wood in the mold of a towering palace with delicately-carved columns and eaves. However, the wooden Tang pagoda is no longer in sight and the visible Ming pagoda had also collapsed during that storm in 1981.

For Buddhists and locals, the fall of the Famen pagoda aroused great sadness and sorrow. They believed for generations the genuine Sarira was buried right under the pagoda. But for archeologists, the collapse of the pagoda provided them a golden opportunity to unveil the secrets of thousands of years. Though historical references indicate there is an underground palace beneath the pagoda and that there are a Buddha's phalanx Sarira and countless treasures, nobody was sure of it.

Soon archeologists cleared out the foundation of the Ming pagoda and then that of the Tang pagoda. When the exploration on the Tang foundation went further, people became more and more curious: did the underground palace and Buddha Sarira referred to by folklore and historical references ever exist? If they did, are they still intact? Have they ever been visited by tomb-robbers?

People pushed the gravel away and a hole in the ground was exposed.

Han Jinke:

Since there was no pagoda to cover it, the sun shone directly into the hole. It looked misty and mysterious and spectacular. Right under the cloud of the mist lay the glittering magnificent gold and silver wares.

Though people were still unsure what

exactly these treasures were, they realized a great archeological discovery was about to come to life. The excited archeologists swiftly re-covered the hole and found the proper entrance at the south side of the foundation to the underground palace.

19 bluestone steps stretched to the entrance of the palace. Then appeared a stone gate with mysterious symbols on it. Apparently, they were not Sanskrit of ancient India. They were characters that could not be understood by human beings. To this day, people still have no clue what they mean. Perhaps they are powerful curses to prevent invasion.

Archeologists were not concerned at all with the curse. They skillfully opened the rusted lock on the stone gate. Later on, they found that this lock had been there for 1,113 years.

Behind the stone gate was the long

19 Bluestone Steps Stretching to the Entrance of the Underground Palace

corridor, flooded with a layer of coins. About 20,000 coins were found in total. 13 of them were made from hawksbill, the first discovery of its kind in Chinese numismatics history.

At the end of the corridor was another stone gate. Standing in front of it were two steles chiseled with Chinese characters.

Itemized Stele

One stele recorded stories of King Asoka distributing Sarira to Famen Temple and Chinese emperors, especially Tang emperors paying tribute to the Sarira. On the other, there was a list of detailed offerings to the Buddha, the quantity of the offerings, and names of the contributors.

These two steles had proven that the mysterious Buddha Sarira and numerous other treasures do exist. But are they really here in this underground palace?

The stone gate behind the stele was hard to open due to distortion of the structure inside.

Han Wei

Former Head of Shaanxi Provincial Archaeology Bureau

When we uncovered the palace, we found the floor stones were all jutting upward. The ceiling was broken too. The stones on the ceiling were dangling over our head. We crawled in. it was very dangerous. So sometimes we worked alone. Sometimes in pairs. While one was working, the other would take care of the situation to make sure no incident would occur. Besides we must be responsible for the artifacts. So the work was really tough.

Although the underground palace's floor and ceiling were distorted by the pressure of the pagoda, earthquakes, and the erosion of time, articles stored within, to every archeologist's amazement, were still as they were originally and kept intact. Among them is this craftwork, as bright and lively as it was a thousand years ago. Experienced scholars immediately recognized that this was a miniature King Asoka pagoda. It was made out of a whole piece of white marble. Bodhisattva figures were chiseled around it. The color of the figures' vermeil skirt and light green belt were so clear and fresh that it seemed they were painted just recently.

Around the miniature pagoda were piles of silkwork. Though the color had faded due to the erosion of time, the delicate design and fine stitches reflected the splendor and delicacy of Chinese ancient silk industry. What excited archeologists even more were some silk clothes found in a white vine box.

Han Wei:

We used to have no knowledge at all about the Tang imperial silk. This time we found this box and 780 layers of silks. If fully unwrapped, these silks would be 400 meter long. They include several hundred clothes. Some belonged to the Queen Mother Hui'an. Wu Zetian's skirt was among them too.

According to the list on the stele, archeologists found all the named articles. This made them believe this silk-work was

Chinese Archaeological Discoveries

The King Asoka Pagoda

Empress Wu Zetian of the Tang Dynasty

Dr Andrica

German Silk Preservation Specialist

Before I worked on this silkwork, I had another piece of silk to experiment with. I used this machine to dampen and dry the silk. The results were excellent.

To Dr Andrica, the restoration is a chance to create. She must carefully analyze the lines and designs of the silk. As for the parts which are not restorable, she has to employ her own perception and imagination to make it up through modern technology.

Dr Andrica:

This column of clothes was superposed in piles when it was not buried here in the Tang dynasty. The back of the column, about 4 cm thick, has been carbonized.

In unwrapping layer after layer, carbonized silk-work needs tremendous patience and care. Sometimes unwrapping one or two layers would take a year. But Dr Andrica has enjoyed her work and has been confident and enthusiastic about it.

Dr Andrica:

While working, I found out how subtle and delicate the ancient, especially Tang, craft-making technology was, which amazed me so much. The impression the Chinese silk gives the world is that you will never forget it once you cast

from the Tang dynasty. Among them was this Empress Wu skirt worn by Wu Zetian, the only empress in Chinese history. And this skirt is the only belonging of Wu Zetian's found so far.

Disappointingly, most of the silk-work was either partially or entirely carbonized. In the Silk Preservation Lab of Shannxi provincial Archeology Bureau, we met Dr Andrica, the silk preservation specialist. She has been endeavoring for years on restoration of the silk-work of thousands of years ago.

Empress Wu Zetian's Gold-thread Silk Skirt

your eyes on it. When we deal with the silk, the work itself is a kind of beauty and enjoyment.

From the carbonized silks, people found that 5 pieces of gold-thread silks were intact. What is it that made them succeed in preventing the erosion of thousands of years?

Through microscope, we learnt that these gold threads were actually stretched gold. They are only 0.1 mm thick in average with the finest being 0.06 mm, which is thinner than human hair. This is a miracle that no modern technology could ever achieve. And these golden threads have the miraculous function of protecting the silk from erosion and enabling us to envision the genuine wonder of the Tang silk over a thousand years later.

This mini gold thread silk dress has short sleeves. The cuffs reach only up to the height of the chest. Its design is very much like modern women's wear. In fact, this is the emblematic dress of Tang handmaidens. From the Tang paintings, we can see beautiful handmaidens of the Tang dynasty. They have a round face, twinkling eyes, and towering hairdos. They proudly expose their plump bosoms and soft skin. And the elegant and delicate silk clothes they are wearing make them even more stunning.

The glory, wonder and splendor of ancient Chinese culture is transported to the West through the world-renowned Silk Road, from Xi'an to the Mediterranean coast. And the Tang dynasty was the peak of the Chinese silk industry. Tang silk is number one among the world's silk in terms of quantity, variety, quality and technique. And this statement can be verified by thousands of silk works of over 40 kinds discovered in the underground palace. All these gold-woven and delicately designed silk pieces inspire our imaginations to ponder that remote era of astonishing wisdom.

More astonishment lies in wait behind other closed stone gates. But archeologists decided to first retrieve treasures of the cave found at the beginning, in case the underground palace collapsed suddenly.

The Emblematic Dress of Tang Handmaidens

According to the structure of the discovered corridor and front chamber, this cave was believed to be the back chamber of the underground palace. When archeologists removed the shattered marble cover and entered the cave, they found it full of treasures. 121 pieces of gold and silver articles were found, together with over 400 pieces of jewelry and jades. This reminds people of the ancient description about treasures in the underground palace: the most sublime in the world, the most splendorous on earth. This description is, by no means, an overstatement.

The most astonishing articles among these gold works are these two gilt silver balls, called perfume bags. Fragrant herbs are put in the small bowl within the ball. Once lit, the aromatic air would overflow through the hollowed designs around the ball. During that time, they were hung in the air to purify the air. To prevent the herbs from pouring out, craftsmen set two loops inside the ball to keep the bowl in balance. When the ball rolls, the balance loops roll as well, so that the bowl in the ball keeps its balance. It is the same principle that is in the balancing equipment of a gyroscope.

The Buddhist Wand is believed to be used by Sakyamuni to disperse snakes or pests, and later on became the symbol of

Perfume Bags

Secrets Underground

The Buddhist Wand

Buddhist authority. This 1.96 meter-long gilt silver wand has two loops at its head and 12 small circles around those two loops. It is regarded as the King of the World Wands. From the words on it, we can tell it was made by a craftsman called An, and that 3.1 kg gold and 2.9 kg silver were used. The two loops are surrounded by 12 beautifully carved golden circles. In the core of the loops is the lotus flower throne, the symbol of sanctity. On top of the throne is a pearl, symbolizing wisdom. The subtlety and delicacy of the wand is unparalleled by any Buddhist wares around the world. But whom does it belong to?

Maybe the answer is behind this gate, the third gate of the underground palace. Embossed on the gate are the images of armored warriors. In the world of Buddhism, they are the guards of the religion. But what are they protecting here?

Behind the third gate was the middle chamber of the palace. A giant white marble mausoleum occupied almost the entire chamber. Above the mausoleum were three cassocks woven with golden thread and silk thread. And there was also a pair of gold threaded silk shoes. Apparently, this special arrangement had some meaning. But what was it?

Then, archeologists found a rotten sandalwood box behind the mausoleum. The box was filled with porcelains. They appeared as plain as daily eating ware such as bowls and plates. But after careful study, it was found that their color was by no means plain.

Zhuo Zhenxi

Pottery and Porcelain Specialist

One of the steles in the palace recorded it clearly. The most important were these three words. They mean "Mi Se" porcelains.

Some Tang scholars used to describe this porcelain with beautiful poems. They described it as ice holding the cloud, and the lotus carrying the dew. But the techniques had long been missing. As a result, no people in this modern age had

"Mi Se" Porcelain

"Mi Se" Porcelain

had the privilege to see the real "Mi Se" porcelains. And so this porcelain had become a thousand year old myth.

Zhuo Zhenxi:

As to why they are called "Mi Se" porcelains, there is no agreement. During the Five Dynasty and Ten Kingdom period, the explanation was that these porcelains were only used by imperial families and should not be kept secret. But according to textual research, this explanation is unfounded. Then why is it called "Mi Se"? This is because there is a grass in South China called Mi grass. The color is adopted in porcelain making. This color is a kind of turquoise. And it is also called "the color of a thousand peaks", because it is of a jade green color reminiscent of remote peaks. It is a very bright jade green, which refreshes people's feelings. It is a very elegant color.

China has a long history of making porcelains for several thousands of years. In the Tang dynasty, the porcelain industry reached a fairly high level. Not only did the splendid Tang Tri-Color porcelain appear, but also the lustrous crystal celadon emerged. And the Mi Se porcelain was the masterpiece of the celadon.

The techniques involved in making Mi Se porcelains are very complicated. Every piece is a masterpiece and even more precious than gold or silver. They are only presented to the imperial family as tributes. These Mi Se porcelains discovered in the underground palace not only solved a thousand year old myth, but also enabled us to clearly envision the treasures once owned only by emperors.

In comparison, the ancient Chinese were not good at making glass. But archeologists accidentally found 20 pieces of glasswork in the underground palace of Famen Temple.

Glass was almost as dear as jewelry and diamonds during these days when coal was not widely used. At that time, only people of some Islamic countries mastered the techniques of making wonderful glass. So experts believe that this glasswork was from exotic countries outside China.

The line designs on this glass are typically Islamic. Line-carved glass was quite popular in the early years of the Islamic region. But it is still rather rare to find such a well-preserved piece as this.

This glass plate is regarded as the world oldest Islamic colored glazed glass so far.

The Islamic Colored Glazed Glass Plate

The Tang dynasty was a very liberal time in Chinese history. Xi'an, then called Chang'an, would hold ceremonies every day to receive guests from all over the world. From this Tang mural painting, we can learn that the Tang imperial court treated foreigners very well, with courteous reception. Businessmen, scholars and ambassadors from all over the world would gather at Chang'an. They brought with them the cultures of their own countries and became messengers of the Tang culture at the same time.

At the underground palace, there is always some new finding to keep people in a state of constant excitement. Archeologists found this tea set with the name WuGe on it. WuGe was the nickname of the 18th Tang emperor, Emperor Xi Zong. Having written his nickname on it indicated how much the emperor cherished this tea set.

Xie Caili
Archaeologist

By the words on the article, we can tell it belonged to Tang Emperor Xi Zong. He offered it to Buddha. All of them are daily wares.

Tea culture blossomed in the Tang dynasty. People during that time were not drinking but eating tea. They first gound the tea into powder, then filtered it with a sifter, added water and spice, and boiled it

The Daily Wares for Drinking Tea by Emperor Xi Zong

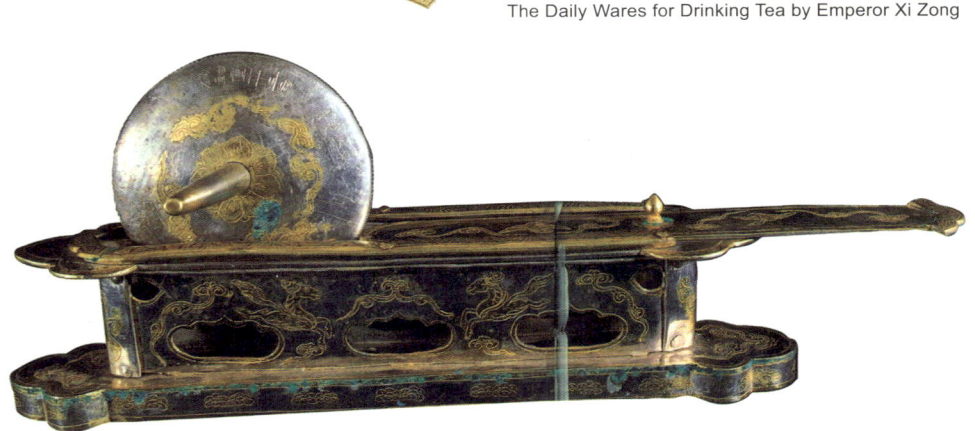

The Ware Used as Grinding the Tea into Powder

on a stove. Finally, the tea would be poured into a glass or porcelain cup for one's appreciation. And this is the whole process of typical imperial Tang tea making, which is rarely known to the world today.

You might wonder why there are so many tea utensils in the underground palace and what special meaning tea has in the world of Buddhism.

According to the monks of the Famen Temple, virtuous hierarchs, elegant scholars and even lofty marquis or emperors associated

The Innermost Casket with a Jade Sarira

tea drinking to religious devotions. And according to Buddhism, tea is regarded as an article of sanctity for Buddha.

It seems that everything in the underground palace is associated with Buddha. Together with the Mi Se porcelain, colored glazed articles, tea sets, and a gilt Bodhisattva statue, fully decorated with jewelry, were carefully positioned in a box. The Bodhisattva's towering hairdo and stunning crown shine a light of holiness. In her hand she carries the lotus leaves, a symbol of sanctity. A silver inscribed tablet is on the top of the lotus leaves. The inscription defines her the Sarira-bearing Bodhisattva. Did she really have a mission to hold the Sarira, a part of Buddha's genuine body?

The excavation was nearly at its end. Only the King Asoka pagoda in the front chamber, the white marble mausoleum in the middle chamber and a silk package in the back chamber were yet to be opened. Archeologists tried carefully to unknot the partially carbonized package. Two hours later, they finally succeeded, and there appeared to be a superposed treasure casket. The outermost one, made of sandal-wood was partially rotten. The others were either made of gold, silver, jade or decorated with numerous jewelry. Altogether 8 treasure caskets were superposed above one another. What is hidden in the innermost casket is a pure gold miniature pagoda with four gates.

The Sarira-bearing Bodhisattva

Chinese Archaeological Discoveries

The Caskets Being Superposed above One Another

Han Wei
Former Head of Shaanxi Provincial Archaeology Bureau

I touched the top of the gold pagoda and found it was movable. Then I uncovered the top and discovered a white pipe-like item was circling around the silver pole within the pagoda. This surprised everybody at the site. What was this? I remembered on one stele it said the Buddha Sarira was about 1.2 inches, the upper edge was smooth with the lower part curving, there were lines on two sides and its color was like white jade but a little greenish, and the bone cave was a little square and had marks in it. I had another look at the pipe-like item and realized the Buddha Sarira had been found.

Coincidentally, the time of discovery was 1 AM in the morning of May 5th 1987, the birthday of Buddha according to the ancient eastern calendar. It was just at this time that the Sarira, believed to exist for thousands of years, described in the ancient references and worshiped by Buddhists around the world, finally appeared from the underground palace of Famen Temple.

However, after careful examination, the Sarira was found to be a fake one made of jade. Did this mean the genuine Sarira did not exist at all? While the disappointment edged in, a young archeologist discovered by accident a coat of floating dirt in the back chamber. They swept away the dirt and a secret box appeared. Within it was a small package and another rusted iron casket. Why had this plain-looking iron casket been so secretly hidden?

Opening up the iron casket, there were more caskets superposed. The silver casket appeared first. Then the sandal casket. Then a mini crystal coffin decorated with giant jewelry, and a clean, smooth jade coffin. Finally, a Buddha phalanx was discovered, laying quietly in wait.

At the sight of this, the people at Famen Temple must have started their worshipping. This bone Sarira was no doubt the sacred Buddha Sakyamuni's phalanx.

Following this, archeologists found two other jade Buddha Sarira in the white marble mausoleum and the King Asoka pagoda. Though nobody quite understood why there existed one bone Sarira and three jade Sariras, the discovery of the genuine Sarira itself was a great source of excitement in the Buddhist world.

Three Jade Sariras

Secrets Underground

The Excavation Site of Genuine Sarira Discovered

Zhi Hui

Renaissanee of Famen Temple

According to historical references, there is only one Buddha's phalanx in the world, which is the one found in Famen Temple. It is not like other Sariras, which are distributed to different places and all of a certain type. There are two Buddha's teeth, for example. One is in Lingguang Temple. The other in Sri Lanka. Some other Sariras of Buddha's body are found constantly in countries world wide. But the phalanx Sarira is the only one in the world.

At this point, the true meaning of all treasures in the palace had been discovered. All this splendor and luxury were offered to worship this unparalleled Sarira. With the secrets of the underground palace uncovered, a world that existed so long ago could be clearly pictured.

Buddhism was first introduced into China in the Eastern Han dynasty, in around the 1st century. But only in the Tang dynasty had it reached its peak. People had then entrusted their life to Buddha. Even emperors prayed to Buddha for social stability and national prosperity. And with the emperors' support, the Tang hierarch Xuanzang ventured tens of thousands of miles on foot and reached India after 15 years of hardship and travel. He carried back with him large amounts of Buddhist scriptures. When Buddhism started fading in India, it took root in China and thrived. Meanwhile, it enriched Chinese poems, music, paintings, sculptures, architecture, novels, and even the Chinese language.

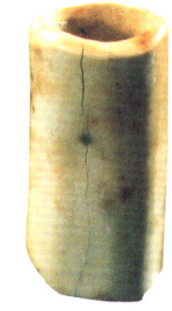

Buddha Sakyamuni's Phalanx

The Buddhist Sculpture

Wu Limin

Director of Research Institute of the Buddhism Culture of China

Buddhism has already penetrated into every corner of Chinese culture and become a very important part of its tradition. If you entirely reject Buddhism, then you might not even be able to speak properly. Many Chinese words are derived from Buddhism.

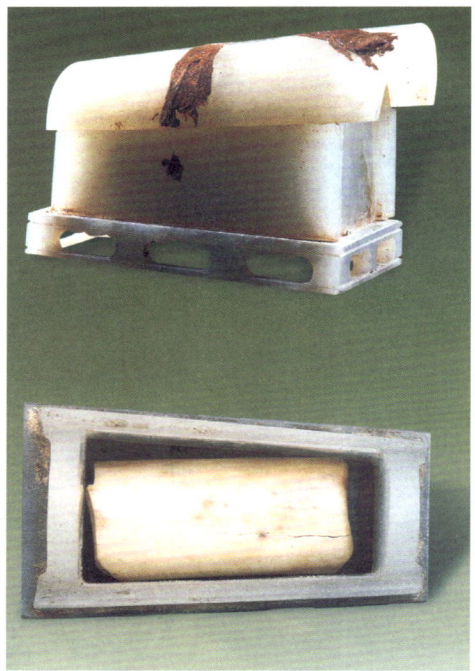

A Clean, Smooth Jade Coffin with a Buddha Phalanx

In the Tang dynasty, people believed a fable. It said that the Famen pagoda only opened once every 30 years and if the Buddha Sarira could be displayed, the country would be prosperous and people would be rich and happy. Li Shimin, the second emperor of Tang, ordered to open the Famen pagoda in 632 AD and led his people to worship the Sarira and pray for safety and happiness. This event set an example for more ardent Buddha worshipping events later on. As a result, Famen Temple became one of the grandest and most honorable temples of the nation. According to historical references, Famen Temple at that time had 24 courtyards and accommodated thousands of monks.

Among artifacts of the underground palace are clothes, belongings, and even the hairs of Tang emperors, including the Empress Wu Zetian. And these unique, stunning treasures with characters 'made upon the emperor's order' verify the historical events of Tang emperors that called for and worshipped the bone of Buddha.

In fact, during the 300 plus years of the Tang dynasty, 6 Tang emperors had called for and worshipped the bone of Buddha. Every time the Famen pagoda was opened, it would arouse people's religious zeal and feverish ardor. Not only were the emperors offering the most luxurious and most cherished belongings to the Buddha, so would the civilians be kneeling for a glimpse of the Sarira at any cost.

However, Emperor Wu Zong, the fifteenth Tang emperor, was not so fond of Buddhism. When he came in power, he forbade all Buddhist activities and ordered to destroy the Buddha's phalanx.

Han Jinke
Head of Fufeng Cultural Bureau and one of the participants of the excavation. He was the first to discover the secret underneath the pagoda.

During the five years between 841 AD and 845 AD, campaigns of exterminating Buddhism have been all over the country. Famen Temple was severely damaged. According to characters on this stele, Emperor Wu Zong ordered Sarira to be carried to the court and crushed in front of him. A monk of Famen Temple risked his life to keep the Sarira and produced a fake one to keep the emperor in the dark.

The 4 Sariras found in the underground palace verified this statement. Only one of them is the real Buddha's bone. The other three are only jade replications. The jade

Miniature of 24 Courtyards of Tang Famen Temple

Sariras serve as protection of the real one. On the other hand, they are the real Sarira's shadows. It is as if the real Sarira is the moon and the other three are shadows of the moon.

Although the Buddhism-extermination campaigns had halted due to regime changes, the Tang empire had already passed its golden period and started waning. The 17th Tang Emperor Yi Zong was the last Tang emperor to open the Famen pagoda in 873 AD, in order to pray for blessing from the Buddha. However, the emperor died during the worshipping ceremony. His successor was only 12, known as Tang Xi Zong with the nickname Wu Ge. The first thing he did was to return Buddha's bone to Famen Temple.

It was a day in 874 AD. People were hurling coins into the underground palace, crying breathlessly. With the giant iron lock clinching the last stone gate, the 242 year-old tradition of calling for and worshipping the Buddha's bone had ended. The treasures and the Sarira were buried forever in

The Buddhist Sculptures

the underground palace. And they were kept intact until 1,113 years later when archeologists reopened the palace.

Han Wei
Former Head of Shaanxi Provincial Archaeology Bureau

This was a chance of a lifetime. If you happened to be there, then you were somewhat connected to those imperial events. For then did one emperor call the bone of Buddha out, the other returned it back. These two events had a unique historical and perhaps, metaphysical connection.

Although the Tang dynasty had been off the stage of history 30 years after the underground palace was closed, it was no doubt one of the most mysterious and prosperous dynasties in Chinese history. And it was a dynasty all Chinese would be proud of. It left behind not only its extraordinary civilization but also countless astonishing treasures, including the sacred Buddha's phalanx which so many Tang emperors had been enamored with.

The Sarira's reemergence after its over 1000 year-old slumber in the underground palace excited Buddhists all over the world. In spring of 2002, the Sarira was asked for in Taiwan to accept the worship from Taiwanese Buddhist followers and ordinary people. The thousand year wait was worthwhile. Maybe the extraordinary ceremonies and ardent worshipping are destined to re-occur in modern times.

But life in the temple is as plain as usual. Despite a thousand years of vicissitude, monks keep their way of life as simple as possible, reciting the inscriptions to the soft sound of bells in the morning and worshipping the Buddha in a solemn, reverent mood.

The world of Buddhism is full of myth and secrets. When the treasures of the underground palace were transferred to well-built museums, people realized that

Secrets Underground

The Sarira of the Buddha

Ceremonies Held in Taiwan to Worship the Phalanx Sarira of the Buddha

more puzzles were yet to be solved. Why were the walls of the underground palace painted in secretive black? Why have Bodhisattva's images been carved at any space available on a Buddhist ware? Why do these Bodhisattvas appear different from ones of other Buddhist temples? It seems every single treasure is arrayed into a particular position in a certain pattern. But what is this pattern and what does it mean?

Han Jinke
Head of Fufeng Cultural Bureau and one of the participants of the excavation. He was the first to discover the secret underneath the pagoda.

There is a pattern. But what it means is not clear yet. We can only say it is an unique, unparalleled religious pattern to worship the Buddha.

As with any other religion in the world, Buddhism has different branches. Esoteric Buddhism is one of them. It is a branch full of mysteries and has profound principles, complicated rules, and mystic ways of succession. Tibetan Lama religion is a branch of Esoteric Buddhism but different from the one that prevailed during Tang dynasty.

Today, Tibetan Esoteric Buddhism still has a large group of followers. But Tang Esoteric Buddhism has vanished in China, apart from branches transferred to Japan and South Korea. Hence, a broken link in Chinese culture had occurred. Fortunately, the archeological excavation in Famen underground palace has fixed the link and brought the Tang Esoteric Buddhism back to China from its 1,000 year long absence.

These astonishing Bodhisattva statues are arrayed in a certain order or pattern. In Sanskrit it is called mandala.

Actually, the mandala is a ritual field that contains the most delicate Buddhist

Bodhisattva Statues Arrayed in a Certain Pattern

ritual pieces. In the mandala of Famen underground palace, there are the holiest Buddha's phalanx Sarira, the dearest offerings, the highest-quality burial spaces and the highest-ranked Bodhisattvas. In the words of Buddhism, it gathers essences and it spreads spirits.

Bodhisattva Statues Arrayed in a Certain Pattern

Secrets Underground

Han Jinke
Head of Fufeng Cultural Bureau and one of the participants of the excavation. He was the first to discover the secret underneath the pagoda.

People come to this underground palace not only to kowtow or burn incenses. Every Buddha or Bodhisattva is a symbol of wisdom. According to Esoteric Buddhism, by coming here one may upgrade one's wisdom to the level of Buddha. Everyone can be the Buddha if one's knowledge can reach the level of wisdom of the Buddha.

Religion is a kind of human understanding of the universe and of the things within it. Esoteric Buddhism has its own profound principles and systemic perception of the world. Today, experts are still working on it, trying to solve more of its puzzles. However, to fully discover all the secrets buried under Famen Temple requires more time, effort, and contemplation.

Ancient Music

Legend has it that more than 2000 years ago, a minister in the Chu State revolted and fled to another state called Sui. The angry king of Chu chased the minister with his army. To inspire the soldiers' morale and strike fear into the enemy, the Chu king ordered that a hathpace be built, on which the soldiers beat their war drums and crusaded against the rebel. The small hill has therefore been left with a rhythmic name, "Drum-beating Hill".

The thousand-year-old story has since long faded away. One day in the 1970s, people fortunately discovered near the Drum-beating Hill that there indeed lies an ancient kingdom with wonderful stories and music.

ANCIENT MUSIC

CHINESE ARCHAEOLOGICAL DISCOVERIES

Hubei province in the middle of the far-flung land of China is one of the origins of the ancient Chinese civilization. Up to now, in its capital Wuhan there are still many historical relics.

2500 years ago, this land was the territory of the Chu state, one of the seven most powerful states in China.

Suizhou is 155 km northwest of Wuhan. According to the local legend, an ancient kingdom named Sui once built its capital here more than 2000 years ago. The name of Sui stems from here.

The story of the Chu King's pursuit of the rebellious minister took place in the suburbs of Suizhou city. The villagers of the Drum-beating Hill have been accustomed to the surrounding scenery. The legend has passed on from generation to generation. However, no one really knows what kingdom it was.

Wang Jiagui, who had become a soldier in his teens, still comes around every now and then. In his simple life experience, the most memorable stories took place here.

More than 20 years ago, in the autumn of 1977, the army where Wang Jiagui stayed decided to build a workshop. They chose the two small hills near the Drum-beating Hill. After an explosion, there appeared yellow and black soil in the earth. Wang Jiagui found it very strange.

Wang Jiagui

Former vice director of the Radar Maintenance Station of the Air Force in Wuhan
I found this kind of soil very strange, for there was red sandstone all round, and in the middle there was the mixed soil as described in archaeological literature.

In the past, people called this Guanyin soil. This kind of soil can be a sealant and keep out water. This soil was refilled artificially and there were traces of tamping. So I suspected that this was an ancient tomb.

Wang Jiagui's guess was right. After the archaeologists got the news and came to the spot, the experts affirmed, after exploration, that there was indeed an ancient tomb built more than 2000 years ago.

In May, 1978, after nearly 6 months of preparations, the excavation formally began. After shoveling the hard earth surface and thick mixed soil, soft and sticky soil appeared. Its name is blue clay, which is an excellent sealant that can partly isolate the tomb from air and protect organic substances.

Beneath the blue clay there was also a tier of 60,000 kg of charcoals, which was a delight to the archaeologists. Although the specific effect of blue clay and charcoal has not been discovered so far, people once discovered the same kind of blue clay and charcoal in the Mawangdui tomb of the Western Han dynasty in Changsha. Some inferred that it was the soil and the charcoal in the Mawangdui tomb that moistened and prevented the tomb owner's body from decay, making it the best preserved one in the world.

Then, is this carefully protected ancient tomb safe from decay? Is the tomb owner as lucky as the female body in Mawangdui?

Having cleared out the blue clay and charcoal, there appeared a huge wooden lid. People discovered that the outer coffin was built with 171 pieces of rectangular wood. No traces were found of sawing or digging on all the wooden pieces, which shows that they were chopped and cut from complete catalpa trees. The scale of this wooden outer coffin is amazing even to archaeologists.

The Outer Coffin with a Huge Wooden Lid

Early in the morning of May 17, the huge coffin lid was slowly removed. People found that the tomb chamber was filled with turbid mud. There were a couple of coffins floating on the water. Whose resting places were they?

Tan Weisi, a Hubei archaeologist, is the former director of the archaeological team. The excavation of the ancient tomb in Suizhou is the most exciting experience in his archaeological life. He still remembers the first relic unearthed from the tomb.

A Mandarin Duck-shaped Lacquer Suitcase

Tan Weisi

Former director of the archaeological team of the Zeng Hou Yi Tomb

When we began pumping water, something appeared in the water from the western chamber. We called it a headless little duck, because its shape was like a duck without a head. We didn't know whether it was a duck or not.

Later people found its head. It turned out to be a mandarin duck. In Chinese people's minds, mandarin ducks are representatives of faithful love. This is a lacquer suitcase for needles, thread, or cosmetics. Its owner should be a female.

On top of the lacquer suitcase were two strange pictures. Half-human, half-beast monsters are dancing and singing. What are the musical instruments they are playing?

For a long time, the Drum-beating Hill had been a tranquil place far away from big cities. Lush rivers flow on the plain, surrounded by green mountains. Villagers lived a peaceful farming life. However, since the appearance of the ancient tomb, there has been many a change to the villagers' lives.

Today in the field of the village stands a piece of modern architecture, the Drum-beating Hill Site Museum, inside of which is the site of the ancient tomb. Recovery and protection have been going on for more than 20 years, and the wooden pieces of the outer coffin have all been dehydrated.

Although tourists cannot see the abundant burial objects, they can appreciate even more clearly the wonderful tomb architecture beside the empty tomb chambers.

Ancient Music

The Strange Pictures on the Lacquer Suitcase

The tomb is 220 sq m. of the total area and 13 m. deep. The whole tomb is divided into four chambers with the huge wooden coffin pieces. They are the eastern, northern, western and central chambers.

The couple of coffins that floated on the water were placed in the western chamber. Archaeologists discovered, while checking these coffins, that all 13 bodies were women. Later, they found another 8 female bodies beside the tomb owner in the eastern chamber.

It was estimated that these females were about 20, the oldest being only 26 years old and the youngest being 13. Experts think that they were buried with the dead.

Li Tianyuan

Research fellow of the Archaeological Institute of Hubei

This is the skull from the No. 10 coffin in the western chamber. She is the youngest in age.

Why did they die at such a young age? Was it because of war, or conspiracy?

Li Tianyuan:

The bones of the 21 females buried with the owner were basically complete without trace of wounds. So we inferred that they were ordered to commit suicide, and that their deaths weren't painful.

The Outer Coffin

Who knows what those young girls were thinking about? They must have been the favorite concubines of the master. Perhaps it was because of this that they must follow their master even to death. However, who was the master of these girls?

The excavation still carried on. People discovered that this tomb was different from the other tombs excavated in the past. The whole tomb is in the shape of an irregular polygon, which is rather rare among Chinese ancient tombs that deem symmetry as beauty.

33

Tan Weisi
Director of the archaeological team of the Zeng Hou Yi Tomb

Why is this tomb in the shape of a polygon with many chambers? This follows the Chinese traditional burial customs. There's the principle of "death as life", which means that after a man's death, the tomb should be arranged according to his possessions. This shape is actually that of his palace when he was alive. So we call it an underground palace.

10 Round Hoof-like Feet below the Outer Coffin

12 Bronze Knobs on the Lid of the Outer Coffin

What is more unbelievable is that in the 13-meter deep tomb there were no traces of ladders. How were the coffins and burial objects placed in the deep tomb? Had the people at that time already learned to use mechanical equipment?

The eastern chamber, which faces the direction where the sun rises, is the resting place of the tomb owner.

When unearthed, the main coffin was placed in the mid-west area of the eastern chamber and pointed north and south. On the excavation spot, archaeologists found a problem: the whole coffin was skewed to the west. Was this a special custom? After careful examination, they discovered that a copper corner of the outer coffin had been stuck to the wooden wall. What had taken place here?

According to the measurement, people discovered that the scale of the main coffin was amazing. It is 3.2-meter long, 2.1-meter wide, and 2.19-meter high. It is divided into two layers with an inner coffin inside the outer coffin. The engineers estimated that the main coffin might weigh as much as 4 tons. However, archaeologists met with problems when they attempted to elevate the main coffin at the excavation spot.

Tan Weisi:
The first time, we used a crane of 8.5 tons. The coffin wouldn't move. Then we added 5 tons and that didn't work, either. The two cranes could lift a dozen tons, but they didn't work.

People had to remove the lids of the inner and outer coffins, take out the relics first, and make the inner coffin float out with water. The crane thus managed to move the inner and outer coffins out of the tomb. It turned out that the total weight of the coffins was more than 9 tons.

Chen Zhongxing

Research fellow of the Hubei Museum

It is the biggest and the heaviest coffin in the world. It was made of bronze and wood, which is unprecedented. How was it made? First, a U-shape bronze framework was made and wooden pieces were embedded inside. The lid was also made of bronze.

The decoration on the outer coffin is not so impressive. However the designer was so careful that he opened a hole in the lower part of the outer coffin. Some inferred that this perhaps was for free in and out passage for the master's soul.

How did the people manage to lower the 9-ton coffin into the tomb over 2000 years ago? There are 12 bronze knobs on the lid of the outer coffin, and there are 10 round hoof-like feet below it. These perhaps are the places where the ancient people fastened their ropes. People speculate that the huge coffin was hung down the cave with some simple machines. However, in the process of settling down, an accident took place and the coffin lost control and fell down to the west. A bronze corner of the lid of the coffin was therefore stuck to the wooden wall.

Compared with the outer coffin, the inner one is exquisite and magnificent. The coffin was painted with red lacquer from inside out, and on both sides was painted

Complex and Mysterious Decorative Paintings on the Inner Coffin

a window. Around the windows, there are complex and mysterious decorative paintings.

To study these ancient paintings, painters were invited to duplicate the ancients' work.

Fu Zhongwang

Vice President of the Hubei Art Academy

These paintings are very far from us. They are very remote. All these images and lively patterns, including the animals and figures, they are too distant from modern life.

They are both human-like and animal-like. Experts inferred that they were actually celestial beasts that protected the master.

Fu Zhongwang
Vice President of the Hubei Art Academy

Their shapes and colors give you a special, impressive feeling. They are very mysterious. They are so charming that you will want to keep looking at them.

When unearthed, there was also a bronze animal beside the coffins. It has antlers as beautiful as that of a deer and a long neck and wings like a crane. In ancient China, cranes and deer are propitious animals and gods always fly on cranes. Perhaps this crane with deer horns is the celestial bird that flies to heaven with the master.

After thousands of years, is the master still safe and sound?

However, this master is not as lucky as the hostess of the Mawangdui Tomb.

Here are all the bone remains of him.

Li Tianyuan
Research fellow of the Archaeological Institute of Hubei

From the bone sutures, we can infer that here are the coronal suture and sagittal suture, and here is the lambdoid suture. These three major sutures on the top of the skull have been basically recovered. We infer that he is in his forties. To be more exact, he may be 45 years old.

From the remains of the body, we know that the master is about 1.63 meters tall. Because of the relative completeness of the skull bones, the head sculpture of the master was recovered.

This is a short, ordinary-looking man. However, the luxuriant tomb shows that he used to have tremendous power and countless wealth. He must have lived a remarkable life. Who was he?

In the early morning of May 23, 1978, there was an unusually colorful cloud in the sky. This day remained in many people's memory.

At noon, the pump was still pumping the water out and only a few people remained at the site. All of a sudden, Feng Guangsheng, who was in charge of the pump, discovered something.

The Bronze Statue of "Zeng Hou Yi"

Ancient Music

The Chime Bells

A Bronze Animal with Antlers of a Deer and a Long Neck and Wings like a Crane

Feng Guangsheng

Vice President of the Hubei Art Technological Academy

At first I saw that there were three black things under the water. I didn't know what they were and began examining them. As the water gradually fell, I saw three small tiers.

This photo shows a faint shadow. What is it?

When the water was finally pumped out, the spectacle in the central chamber attracted everyone's attention.

There were 65 pieces of bronze chime bells hanging neatly in the wooden tiers, as if buried just recently. Through more than 2000 years, the bells had steadily stood in place, which was unprecedented in world

37

The Inscriptions on the Chime Bells

archaeological history. They are also the most magnificent treasure unearthed in the ancient tomb of the Drum-beating Hill.

The bells stand in the shape of a try square along the western and southern walls of the central chamber. Their total length is over 10 meters.

The bells were hanging in three layers, each layer with bells of different shapes. The chime bells on the upper layer are called Niu Bell, and those on the middle and lower layers are called Yong Bell. The bells vary a lot in size. The lightest bell weighs only 2.4 kg, whereas the heaviest weighs as much as 203.6 kg. The whole set weighs 5 tons.

On the tier there are bronze swordsmen loyally supporting the wooden girder of the tier. They are solemn, respectful, and strong. They resemble guards in the palace.

On the chime bells were inscribed more than 3000 beautiful Chinese ancient characters, including the number, chronicles, marking, and rhythms of the chime bells. This can be called an ancient music course book.

These characters also revealed the identity of the mysterious master. According to the inscriptions, this set of chime bells belonged to "Zeng Hou Yi", that is to say, the name of the master of the tomb is Yi, the king of the Zeng state. No wonder he can possess such a luxuriant underground palace and chime bells.

Before the excavation of the chime bells, there were also some other unearthed chime bells. However, most of them cannot produce any sound. What about the fate of these chime bells?

Feng Guangsheng
Vice President of the Hubei Art Technological Academy

When we first rang the chime bells, everyone was struck by its tone, which was clear as a water drop, and its long resonation. It was so wonderful.

The Bronze Swordsmen Loyally Supporting the Wooden Girder of the Tier

Ancient Music

After that, we tried other bells. We found out that the sound of the small bells was bright and pleasant, and that of the bells in the middle layer was smooth, and that of the lower bells deep and vigorous. In a word, the sound was awe-inspiring to all the musicians present.

The scale of the chime bells equals C major in modern music, and the sound range includes 5 and a half octachords, which is only one octachord fewer than that of the modern piano in alto and bass. In the central range, all the twelve halftones are complete. Theoretically speaking, this is a set of musical instruments that can play all kinds of music and express many complex musical techniques.

More than 2000 years ago, that the ancient Chinese learned such harmonious music, is truly amazing. Zeng Hou Yi chime bells therefore attracted attention from all over the world and became the outstanding representative of ancient Chinese cultural relics.

Since ancient times, the Chinese have cherished a special love for music. Many legends about music have passed on from generation to generation.

In today's Wuhan city, there is such a hathpace for playing the ancient Chinese fiddle. It was said that there was a musician named Boya. He was excellent in playing the fiddle but nobody could understand his music. One day he met a logger named Zhong Ziqi here, who totally understood his music. After Zhong Ziqi's death, Boya was so sad that he crashed his fiddle before Ziqi's tomb and ceased playing ever since.

In ancient China, the Chinese fiddle was a symbol of an elegant life. It is said that playing the fiddle had been popular in China over 3000 years ago. This 2000-year-old ancient fiddle was unearthed from the Zeng Hou Yi Tomb. In fact, Zeng Hou Yi left us with altogether 125 ancient musical instruments.

This set of musical instruments was discovered beside the chime bells. It is called stone chimes. It is made of special stones and its sound is high, clear, and pleasant.

The Hathpace for Playing the Ancient Chinese Fiddle, in Wuhan of Hubei Province

39

The Ancient Chinese Fiddle

Chime bells and stone chimes formed the center of the orchestra. Because ancient Chinese called bronze "gold", the two instruments were referred to together as the "sound of gold and stone". Ancient Chinese people regarded this sound as the most wonderful sound in the world.

Besides these, there are also Se, Jian drum, Chi, panpipe, and others. All these instruments form a complete palace orchestra. In ancient China, palace music was not only for amusement, but more importantly, stood for power, dignity and order.

In Zeng Hou Yi's bedroom there are also some musical instruments, such as fiddles, Se, drums, and panpipes. These musical instruments were perhaps used for playing light music. After a busy day, Zeng Hou Yi could return to his home and listen to romantic music, surrounded by beautiful girls. That may have been the most pleasant moment of his entire day.

Some inferred that the 21 girls buried with him might be the dancers and singers of Zeng Hou Yi. Out of fear of loneliness after death, he may have decided to bring along beautiful singers and dancers to continue his pleasure in life.

This underground palace permeated with ancient music appears peaceful and tranquil. However, the northern chamber in the tomb broke up this tranquility.

This is Zeng Hou Yi's storage room, where a large number of weapons were stored. On many of the weapons there were strange characters inscribed and inlaid with gold. They were still lustrous when unearthed.

This object is called "spear-shaped axle cap". Its head is sharp and looks like a spear, but it is actually a component of the war chariot. In a war, it is fixed at the axis of the chariot and can both strengthen the axle of the chariot and kill the enemy near it.

Ancient Music

Stone Chimes

This group of arrowheads was still very sharp when unearthed and could easily cut through a bundle of letter paper.

Weapons are the most numerous objects in Zeng Hou Yi's tomb. This music-loving master must have also been good at fighting.

Tan Weisi
Director of the archaeological team of the Zeng Hou Yi Tomb

Of the 15,000 cultural relics unearthed from the tomb, most of them are weapons. There are many kinds. Some have long poles and are used for jabbing enemies, others are short weapons, and others are arrows for enemies farther away. Besides, there are also many chariots. From all this, we can see that Zeng Hou Yi was a military commander who excelled at chariot fighting.

A Spear-shaped Axle Cap

41

Arrowheads

The central chamber stands for Zeng Hou Yi's living room. Chime bells were placed on the western and southern sides, and closely placed along the southern wall was the grand feast. Various ritual vessels were placed in good order. It was the first time for archaeologists to see such a well-preserved spectacle.

Among the grave vessels, there is a set called "Nine Ding and Eight Gui". When unearthed, there were still bones of beef, mutton and chicken in Ding, whereas Gui was used to contain corn. They are high-rate ritual vessels for sacrifices to ancestors. Only nobles can use them.

On the basis of this, we can affirm that Zeng State used to be very powerful.

However, these resulting finds puzzled people.

According to the textual research and carbon 14 mensuration, it can be inferred that Zeng Hou Yi died between 433 BC and 400 BC.

It was an age of warfare. The period from the 5th century BC to the 3rd century BC is referred to as the "warring states" in Chinese history. States struggled and fought against each other to expand their territories and power. The heroes of the drama are the powerful kings and non-conformists. What role, then, did Zeng Hou Yi play at that time?

In the central chamber where the chime bells were unearthed, people discovered the dignity of the master.

Wan Quanwen

Vice Curator of the Hubei Museum
So far many bronze wares with inscriptions about the Zeng state have been unearthed in Suizhou, Zaoyang, and Jingshan in Hubei and Nanyang in Henan. The discovery of the Zeng Hou Yi Tomb, shows that in that area should have been a state named Zeng. However, in literature, there are only records of the Sui state.

Ancient Music

A Set of Ritual Vessels Called "Nine Ding and Eight Gui"

No cultural relic has been unearthed about Sui through the many years of excavation. Does the Sui state exist? What is its relation to the Zeng state? Many historians tend to think that Zeng and Sui are actually one country.

Although no record has been found concerning the history of the Zeng state in literature, two piles of bamboo slips provided us some information. The bamboo slips are a list of the burial objects, in which a faithful record has been left about the guests at the burial and the gifts of chariots and weapons.

Besides the people from the Zeng state, the gift presenters were mainly the king, prince, and ministers from Chu state. Among the chime bells unearthed, there is a bell sent by the Chu king. The characters on the bell said that during the 56th year of the Chu king's reign, he had a bell made for sacrifices and presented it to Zeng Hou Yi as a gift. This proves that Zeng and Chu kept close ties.

According to historical literature, Chu used to be the most powerful state. For a long time, it was the strongest state in South China.

The Chime Bell Sent by the Chu King to Zeng Hou Yi

Wan Quanwen
Vice Curator of the Hubei Museum

In its 800-year-long history, the Chu state destroyed over 60 small states. The Zeng state became a dependent state of Chu since the middle of the Spring and Autumn period. However, it was not destroyed by Chu until the middle of the Warring States period. One of the major reasons is that the Zeng state once saved the Chu king. In 506 BC, the Zhuang king of Chu fled to the Zeng state when the Wu army invaded Ying. The Zeng state did honorable service to the Chu king and so was spared by the Chu state.

The Set of Lacquer Wares Used as the Food Vessels for Picnics

None of the inferences can completely identify the history of Zeng state or the life of Zeng Hou Yi. Many place their hope on future archaeological discoveries. In fact, 76 ancient tombs in the Warring States Period have been discovered near the Drum-beating Hill. This is perhaps the cemetery of nobles and civilians of Zeng state. The mysterious Drum-beating Hill is also suspected to be a grand tomb place. Perhaps some day in the future we can discover more secrets about the ancient state.

Although there are still many puzzles, the surprise that Zeng Hou Yi Tomb brought to us has far exceeded original expectations. In this tremendous ancient tomb, there are altogether over 15,000 burial objects. Besides the musical instruments, weapons, and ritual vessels, there are also many utensils. The bronze wares weigh 10 tons. 9 relics were ranked as national-treasure-level relics and many elaborate works are on exhibition in the Hubei Museum.

Lacquer wares are the invention of the ancient Chinese. People first make frames with wooden blocks or planks, then paint lacquer on the outside. Lacquer wares are not only light and practical but also bright and beautiful in color. Up to now they are still very popular art wares. More than 2000 years ago, craftsmen have poured into the lacquer wares many clever ideas. This set of lacquer wares is the food vessels for picnics, which can contain boxes, cans, spoons, and so on. When unearthed, there were still stones of fruits in the box.

Most of the 134 bronze ritual vessels and utensils in Zeng Hou Yi Tomb were placed in the central chamber. They stand for power and luxury.

These two big Zun Fou are wine jars. Despite their plain appearance, they are very practical. Both jars are over 1.2 meters high and weigh more than 600 kg together. It is said that they can contain over 400 kg wine.

These two big pots are also wine containers. To people's surprise, the two pots which weigh over 200 kg were placed on a bronze plank named Jin, and all the weight was supported by the four small beast hooves underneath the plank. Only four such "Twin Hu"s have been unearthed so far and they are regarded as rare treasures.

Another pair of Jian and Fou also attracted people's interest. The bronze Jian and Fou are composed of two parts. The outer part is called Jian and the inner one Fou. There is a margin between Jian and Fou for placing ice pieces. That is to say, this is a set of utensils for icing the wine. Some refer to it jokingly as the ancient refrigerator of China.

This object is the stand for a musical instrument, the Jian drum. When unearthed, the Jian drum decayed. This round hole is where people fixed the Jian drum.

Fu Zhongwang
Vice President of the Hubei Art Academy

On the whole, it looks like a burning fire. When closely examined, it resembles many dragonheads and tails stretching all around. I think that it is a sculpture that truly stands on its own. Although it is the stand of the Jian drum, to me, it is a perfect sculpture.

This stand of the Jian drum is composed of dragons of varied sizes entertwined

Two Big Pots Used as Wine Containers　　　　The Wine Jar Called Zun Fou

together. On the body of the big dragons there are also many small ones. Due to the complexity and subtlety of the structure, up to now people have still not found out how many dragons there are.

This bronze piece of Zun and Pan is composed of a Zun and a Pan. Zun is a wine container, whereas Pan is the container of water or ice. Zun and Pan are decorated all over with fine and complex cubic patterns composed of innumerous small tangling dragons. After careful examinations, experts concluded that these thoroughly carved ornaments are the most complex objects so far unearthed in China and they were cast with the lost-wax method.

Chen Zhongxing
Research fellow of the Hubei Museum

The so-called lost-wax method means to use wax as the mould. After making the wax mould, they painted such fire-resistant materials as quartz sand on the surface and let it dry in the shade. They then baked the mould in a fire and so the wax was melted. The outside became a new mould and we call it a mould in intaglio. They used this mould to cast bronze wares and finally we get the bronze wares.

The lost-wax method is still used in the field of exact casting. Although technologies today have become a lot more advanced than those 2000 years ago, modern people cannot be compared with their ancestors in terms of the complexity

The Bronze Jian and Fou

The Stand of the Jian Drum, with Many Dragonheads and Tails Stretching All Around

The Part of the Bronze Zun and Pan

and exquisiteness of crafts. To duplicate such wonderful wares as Zun and Pan is very difficult even to modern people.

The bronze casting technique as manifested in the chime bells is also amazing. Through such advanced

The Mouth of Zun Decorated with Fine and Complex Cubic Patterns

The Bronze Piece of Zun and Pan Composed of a Zun and a Pan

technologies as lasers, researchers discovered that all the chime bells were cast with complex pottery moulds. Take the most complex middle Yong bell for example: the whole mould was composed of hundreds of pieces of pottery moulds and earth cores and was cast all at once.

Chen Zhongxing
Research fellow of the Hubei Museum

As for chime bells, there should be a strict control of the proportion of tin to achieve the accuracy of pitch and perfection of tonal color. According to our analysis and research, the amount of tin in the bells is between 12% and 14%, and normally about 13% is the best for perfect pitch and tonal color. This proportion is very strict and is close to the strict requirements for proportion in modern art wares.

The duplication of the first set of chime bells took altogether 7 years. After many attempts, people are finally able to produce an exact copy of the original piece. However, some secrets of our ancestors have not been successfully uncovered, despite people's many efforts.

In the bedroom of Zeng Hou Yi, people discovered many such spring-like things. However, the measurement shows that these metals are very soft and have no plasticity. The metal wires are regularly wound around round wooden pillars and look very much like modern electrical wires. Their usage is still a puzzle today.

This is a suitcase unearthed in the eastern chamber. These ancient and mysterious patterns have charmed many people. It is said that the arch-like lid of the suitcase stands for the sky and the rectangular bottom of the suitcase stands for the earth. The painting on the lid is the ancient Chinese people's knowledge about the universe.

CHINESE ARCHAEOLOGICAL DISCOVERIES

The Usage of the Metal Wires, Discovered in the Bedroom of Zeng Hou Yi, Being Still a Puzzle Today

The character of "Dou" in the middle stands for the Big Dipper. Surrounding the character there are 28 strange names arranged clockwise. They are referred to as the 28 constellations. The 28 constellations are an important invention in Chinese ancient astronomy. On the basis of the law that the moon moves around the earth in 28 days and with the reference of the stars, the ancient people divided the sky above the equator into 28 varied parts and each part was a Xiu. In this way they determined the seasons, solar terms, and chronicles so as to guide agricultural production.

However, to carefully paint the constellations on the clothing case may not only be meaningful in astronomical terms; it may have some deeper meaning.

On both sides of the constellations there are also two kinds of monsters. What are they?

Tan Weisi
Director of the archaeological team of the Zeng Hou Yi Tomb

They divided the globe into east, west, south, and north, and marked them with animals and colors. The east is a green dragon, the west a white tiger, the south a red sparrow, and the north a black tortoise. Green, white, red, and black. Everything is here.

The two beasts turned out to be the green dragon and white tiger, which respectively represent the east and west. On one side of the case there is also a bird-like monster, and some think that this represents the red

The Two Beasts on the Lid of the Suitcase Representing the East and West

A Bird-like Monster on One Side of the Case Representing the South

48

The Suitcase with the Arch-like Lid and the Rectangular Bottom

sparrow in the south. However, the other side of the case was painted with black paint without the tortoise that stands for the north. Why?

The key lies right in the constellation picture. Below one of the constellations, there are clearly a couple of ancient characters, "Jia Yin the 3rd day". According to the chronicles, the so-called Jia Yin the 3rd day refers to May 3rd in 433 BC according to the Chinese traditional calendar. Some experts think that at the dusk of that day, the seven constellations of the north were hidden under the horizon and therefore cannot be seen.

The secret of the case is revealed. The painting turned out to be a picture of the astronomical phenomenon at the dusk of May 3rd, 433 BC.

This must have been an important moment in Zeng Hou Yi's life. However, no one knows exactly what it means.

Unquestionably, Zeng Hou Yi is a hero of his time, but was unfortunately forgotten by the Chinese ancient historians. No one knew when his kingdom began, what achievements he had made, and what troubles he used to have, nor where his posterity had gone and when his kingdom disappeared.

The reason that he deserves our best appreciation is that because of his attachment to life and music, he left us innumerous rare treasures and the wonderfully resounding sound of ancient music.

The Legend of Mawangdui

Over 30 years ago, on a plain in the eastern suburb of Changsha, capital city of Hunan province, there stand two strange mounds. The local folks call these two saddle-like mounds protruding on the field "Mawangdui". They are said to be a tomb of some Wang family in the 9th century.

Are they really tombs? If they are, who were buried in them?

Chinese Archaeological Discoveries

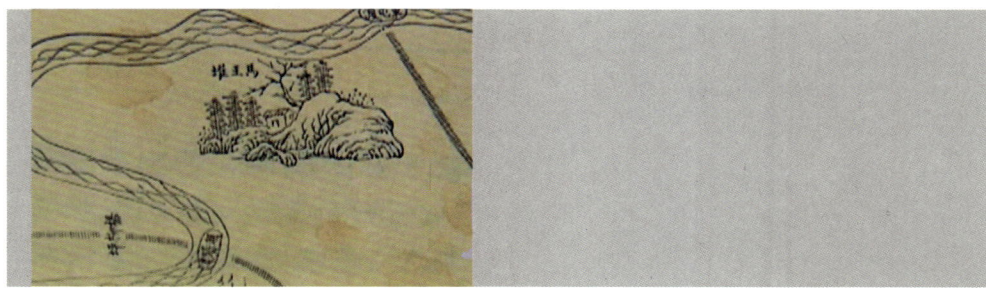

Changsha, capital city of Hunan, is a famous city in South China with a history of over 3000 years. Regretfully, during World War II, a great fire burnt down almost all the ancient architectures on the surface. However, under the ground of this city many precious cultural relics are still preserved.

These two mounds in the eastern suburb of Changsha were referred to by the local folks as "Ma'andui" due to their resemblance to saddles. Later the epithet was misrepresented as "Mawangdui". According to maps, it is a family tomb of Ma Yin, king of Chu State during the Five Dynasties and Ten Kingdoms. What are they and what happened?

At the end of 1971, the local troops planned to construct an underground hospital with the two mounds of Mawangdui. However, in the course of the construction, landslides occurred from time to time. While the workers were probing the underground with drills, a pungent gas came out from the drill hole. Some tested it with fire, and a mysterious blue flame immediately came forth.

Mr. Hou Liang of Hunan Museum was among the first ones who received the news. He immediately realized that the workers came across an ancient tomb. The local dialect calls such tombs fire-pit tombs. It is said that generally in such tombs the relics may be preserved in sound condition. However, when Mr. Hou Liang arrived at the spot, three days had passed since the emergence of the fire.

Hou Liang

Former director of the Mawangdui Excavation Team

At that time I went to the clinic and borrowed a small oxygen bag. I wanted to preserve some of the gas, which had been emitting for 3 days. And during the 3 days, some dozen people were digging. So when I held the bag to the hole, the air bubbles were tiny. Pow-pow, like that. It took me a long time to take in just a little gas. At that time it was turning dark, so I gave up. However in the later research, this was the only thing we lacked. What on earth is this gas? So the absence of this gas is a great pity.

In January, 1972, the archaeological team carried out a formal scientific excavation on the mysterious tomb. After the bulldozer cleared up part of the mound, the tomb entrance emerged, which showed that it was a large ancient mausoleum that measures 20 meters from north to south and 17 meters from east to west.

The further clearage work should be carried out manually. The excavation trudged on in the moist and rainy weather in Changsha.

Bad news came when people were expectantly persisting in the arduous job. A round hole dug by tomb plunderers was discovered.

The hole was directed towards the lower part of the tomb. It was constantly in the way of the excavation work.

Hou Liang
Former director of the Mawangdui Excavation Team

Every day while carrying out dirt, I could see the dark hole. Perhaps because of an iron mine in the earth, the hole looked dark and sooty. Well, I said, what bad luck. Perhaps we spent our utmost strength to dig, only to find out that the tomb was empty.

Stretching 17 meters underneath, the hole finally disappeared. Just at this time, people dug out a glutinous earth. It is popularly known as white paste mud. In the tombs of the South China, such mud has often been used to protect the tombs. It is said to have a good sealing effect. An interesting incident took place at the excavation site. A member claimed that

The Two Mounds Called Mawangdui

he dug out a green leaf from the mud. The surrounding people did not believe that it was an ancient leaf and said it must have fallen down from the tree a moment before.

Fu Juyou
Former vice curator of Hunan Museum

With over a hundred pairs of eyes as witness, we shoveled the mud. The thick mud was shoveled into the dustpan and the basket. Half of the leaf remained in the mud there, and the other half was shoveled down. Everyone said, "It's green!"

Is it really an ancient leaf? This is amazing.

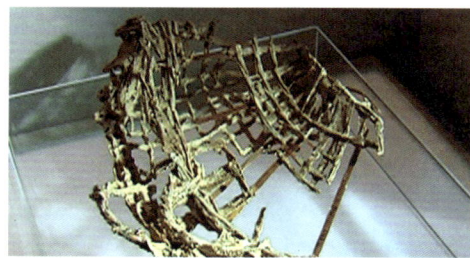

A Yellowish Green Bamboo Basket

In the ensuing excavation, the archaeologists discovered successively some green bows and yellowish green bamboo baskets. Everything was so astounding. They had an expectation that there would be more delightful surprises hidden in this tomb.

There was a thick layer of black charcoal under the white paste mud. It filled 4 trucks and was estimated to exceed 5000 kilograms in weight.

Fu Juyou:
After clearing up the white charcoal paste, we discovered a big bamboo mat.

Hou Liang
Former director of Mawangdui Excavation Team

When we removed the mat, we found this. What a surprise! Some of the senior workers, who had been excavating tombs since before the Liberation said that they had never seen such a well-preserved tomb in their life. Since nine out of ten ancient tombs in Changsha had been robbed before the Liberation, it was really a wonder that this tomb had been in such perfect condition.

This is a square tomb 20 meters deep. From top downward, it narrows like a funnel. At the bottom of the funnel-like tomb there lies a 4-meter-long, 1.5-meter-high tomb chamber. Such an unusually spacious tomb chamber stunned even experienced archaeologists. The chamber was assembled with scores of whole wooden planks, and some of the planks weighed over half a ton.

The extraordinary bulk of the chamber also posed trouble to the team. It was unlikely for them to directly remove the

The Legend of Mawangdui

chamber from the pit. They had to remove the thick and solid planks first inside the tomb.

As soon as the planks were removed, archaeologists realized that their several months of hard labor was not spent over nothing.

This is a huge underground treasure house. In the center lies the tremendous coffin, while the surrounding wing rooms were filled with sparkling treasures. Beneath the mud, every object looked brand new.

Another amazing incident appeared when the archaeologists were carefully

A Huge Coffin Chamber Resembling the Chinese Character "Jing" "井"

picking up the relics. In the eastern wing room this beautiful lacquer utensil was discovered. When the lid was opened, everyone gasped with eyes wide open.

The Excavation Spot of the Square Tomb

Chinese Archaeological Discoveries

Hou Liang
Former director of Mawangdui Excavation Team

When the lid was removed, gosh, there were slices of lotus root covering the water inside it. Alas, Mr. Wang Yuyu from Beijing shouted out, 'Look at that!' The 2000-year-old lotus roots are still in good shape.

At his remark, people crowded to have a look at the rare phenomenon. He was afraid lest the relic be damaged, so he held the vessel and walked slowly to the center and hastened to take a picture of it.

However, as he was taking it to the center, there were only a few pieces left. When he hastened to put it in the car, the lotus root slices were all gone, having turned into a soup.

The Lacquer Utensil

What on earth has preserved in good shape such things that were the easiest to rot away? And what had caused such a wonder to disappear instantly? People at that time had no time to ponder about these confounding mysteries.

The numerous cultural relics were removed out of the pit, and at last, only the master's own resting place was left.

Upon the start of the excavation, there had been various guesses as to the identity of the master of the tomb. However, no convincing proof has been found yet. Who might be buried here?

In such a huge tomb where lotus roots and leaves had been preserved intact and the burial lacquer wares looked brand new, what other wonders might be unfolded?

People waited anxiously for the moment of the opening of the coffin.

The process of the opening of the coffin was again beyond people's expectations. There were four layers in the capacious coffin, and it was only in the innermost

The 2000-year-old Lotus Root Slices in a Lacquer Utensil

layer that the remains of the master of the tomb were preserved. The inner coffin was covered with a mysterious T-shaped silk painting.

This huge, 2-meter-long, intact silk painting was the first discovery of its kind in Chinese archaeological history. What secrets of the master do the complex image in the painting reveal? Why was it placed on the top of the inner coffin, which is the nearest to the remains of the master?

There was no time to seek the answers to these problems. People decided to open the inner coffin in the pit first.

When the inner coffin was opened, there emerged something wrapped tightly with silk. The mysterious tomb master did not show up yet.

In order to better protect the cultural relics, archaeologists took great trouble to move the master of the tomb, together with the coffin, to the museum.

The huge, four-layer coffin was made with quality natural wood. There were altogether 70 planks in the coffin, and all the layers were stuck together with mortises and tenons through exquisite workmanship.

The outermost layer was the solemn black lacquer coffin. It was painted with black lacquer without any ornaments.

The Second-layer Coffin

The Cloud Patterns and Bizarre Beasts or Celestial Beings Painted on the Second-layer Coffin

The second layer was a color-painted lacquer coffin. On the black background were painted with golden paint various cloud patterns, between which were inserted 111 bizarre beasts or celestial beings. With its rich imagination and rugged strokes, the design is permeated with the mystery of the ancient times.

The third layer was a color-painted lacquer coffin. On the red background, there were painted various auspicious designs with green, brown, yellow, and other colors. There were altogether six dragons, three tigers, three deer, one phoenix, and a celestial being. Compared with the outer coffins, this layer was especially magnificent.

The Third-layer Coffin

The innermost coffin was painted with black lacquer and decorated with silk and embroidery. It was the first time that archaeologists discovered a coffin with such decorations.

To see the face of the master, they should remove the outward wrapping silk first.

Hou Liang
Former director of Mawangdui Excavation Team

There were two layers of quilts covering her body. They were very beautiful with bright colors and looked brand new. Alas, we were all very surprised. Mr. Wang Yuyu, as I mentioned just now, who specialized in ancient silk, had never seen such good silk preserved for over 2000 years.

He was overwhelmed with joy. However, when he reached for the silk, something went wrong. The silk could not be removed. They were as soft as tofu. It looked in sound shape but actually had rotted away.

It took them a good week to remove the silk on the master's body. There were 20 pieces of clothes on the master's body, a complete set of silk and hemp clothes for all seasons. In the course of their work, there was a strong sour smell. If the body had been completely rotted away, how could it still emit such a smell?

Zhou Shirong

Former vice director of Mawangdui Excavation Team

We stayed there every day, and the body gave off such a strong odor.

Would there be a wonder indeed? People were waiting anxiously for the answer.

Bai Rongjin

Expert of the Archaeological Institute of Chinese Academy of Social Sciences

The Innermost Coffin

It was already after midnight. I came at 10 o'clock and worked till the latter half of the night to about 3 o'clock. We cut and cut until we arrived at the top of a piece of hemp cloth. I felt beneath the hemp cloth and found something soft.

The master revealed herself, which astounded everyone on the spot.

Zhou Shirong
Former vice director of Mawangdui Excavation Team

There was a body! Next, we should pause, and not act in a haste. Our first task was to solve this problem. What a great discovery!

After being antisepticised, the female body was sent to Hunan Medical College.

She was not like an ancient body. Her skin was still pale yellow and was even elastic when pressed. Some joints were still flexible. When injected with the antiseptic, her parenchyma plumped up and diffused gradually, which was very similar to fresh bodies.

This is not only a wonder in world archaeological history but also a wonder in human history. The immortality of the female body of Mawangdui has ever since become a question constantly under exploration.

By this time, the excavation work of the tomb had been almost completed, but the identity of the tomb master was still a mystery. In the course of the clearage of the relics, people discovered a seal on which was inscribed the characters "Concubine Xin Zhui", which showed that the name of the tomb master was Xin Zhui.

Besides, some burial objects were sealed with such characters as "Chamberlain of Marquis Dai" and "Marquis Dai's Mansion". According to the historical records, Dai was a marquis at the beginning of the Western Han Dynasty and was the former Prime Minister of the Changsha State. So it has been roughly confirmed that the date of the tomb was the beginning of the Western Han Dynasty, and that the chorography of current maps were disproved in that the mounds were not the tomb of the King of Chu State in the Five Dynasties and Ten Kingdoms.

Then, was the tomb master the wife of Marquis Dai? After all, Dai was just an inferior marquis possessing 700 households, whereas the luxury of the tomb was not likely to belong to a wife of such an inferior marquis.

The after-death world of Ms. Xin Zhui is a huge coffin chamber that resembles the Chinese character of jing "井". At the center of the chamber lies the four-layer coffin set, surrounded by numerous burial objects. They have recorded down almost all the wealth and rank of the master before her death.

The Seal Inscribed the Characters "Concubine Xin Zhui"

The front wing room in the north symbolizes her luxuriant sitting room, which is covered with bamboo mats and surrounded with silk curtains. The well-trained handmaids served her attentively, and are symbolized with 23 exquisitely carved wooden figurines.

"Xin Zhui"

Among all the wooden figurines, there is one peerless beauty that attracted the most attention. Her face is exquisitely carved with infinite charms and at the corner of her lips emerges a half smile. When exhibited in the Netherlands, she was crowned as the "Oriental Venus".

The skillful female musical performers are now playing wonderful music for the master. The shape of the figurines provides us with a true scene of the ancient orchestra and gives us some idea about the luxury in which Ms. Xin Zhui indulged herself.

The front wing room resembles the master's bedroom. The incense burners bring the room a wonderful fragrance.

In the room there lies a short lacquer table, with a whole set of dishware on it. It includes five dishes, a bowl of soup, a bowl of wine, and several barbecues, as if it were waiting for the mistress.

The wing rooms on the east, west, and south are all warehouses of Ms. Xin Zhui, where beautiful clothes and abundant materials were stored. The bamboo-plaited baskets and pottery jars were filled with various grain seeds, vegetable seeds, and fruits. Most of them were well preserved when unearthed. There were scores of varieties including paddy, wheat, barley, date, plum, and waxberry, and more. This indicates the booming agriculture of South China at that time.

Why was this woman buried in such a magnificent tomb? So graceful and noble, with so high a social status, she must be Madame Daihou. Why was her body preserved so well over such a long course of two thousand years?

After the female body was unearthed, in order to have a fuller picture of the physical conditions of this body, archaeologists decided to carry out an anatomy on the body after careful discussions. The medical experts of Hunan province were invited to anatomize the body, and the operator was a young doctor named Peng Longxiang.

Exquisitely Carved Wooden Figurines

The Wooden Figurine Crowned as "Oriental Venus"

Peng Longxiang

Professor of Xiangya Medical College of Mid-South University

It can be said that every department of the clinic participated in this anatomy, such as the radiation sector, the dermal sector, the mouth sector, the gynecological sector, the internal medicine sector, the surgery sector, and even the E.N.T. department. So nearly every sector took part in the anatomy. We said jokingly that only the pediatric department did not participate, because the body was an adult.

The anatomy indicates that the female body suffered from various diseases before death, including coronary heart diseases, gall stones, Japanese schistosomiasis, intervertebral disc herniation or distortion between the fourth and the fifth lumbar vertebras, a fracture in the right arm, and so on. She died at the age of 50 or so. The smooth skin shows that she did not suffer too long from the diseases but died suddenly. This aroused people's suspicion: did she kill herself?

Peng Longxiang:

If she had committed suicide, her neck would have been broken, which can be detected either in the examination or in the X-ray photos. So we can see that there is no trace of suicide.

Doctors also found residues of mercury. Did she die from calculated murder? However, scientists held that such little mercury was not so fatal to cause her death.

The noblemen of the Western Han Dynasty liked to take the so-called "celestial pills", which were made with natural minerals. They contained a small quantity of mercury and did more harm than good to the body.

Then, what did she die of?

People discovered 138 and a half pieces of melon seeds that had not been digested. That is to say, she had eaten many melons in less than a day before her death. She must have been a gluttonous woman devoted to sweet food. Did her gastronomy contribute to her death?

People thought about the various animal skeletons, including those of beasts, fowls and fishes, which they discovered in her tomb. Most of them were the food of the mistress. Xin Zhui must have been very particular about her food.

Peng Longxiang
Professor of Xiangya Medical College of Mid-South University

She had many kinds of animal meat among the burial objects, showing that she had a surplus of diet. Such a diet can lead to coronary diseases.

The doctors had another close examination of the physical conditions of Xin Zhui. They discovered that she had gall stones and one of the stones stuck to the entrance of the duodenum. Taking in too many melons may cause gallbladder angina, meanwhile, Xin Zhui also suffered from serious coronary heart diseases with 70 percent of her aortas obstructed. The doctors therefore inferred that she died from the coronary heart diseases induced by gallbladder angina.

It is also unprecedented in archaeological history to have such a clear knowledge of the cause of the death over 2000 years ago. This has largely resulted from the good shape of the body. The anatomy shows that there were only symptoms of earlier stage decay. That is to say, when the body was temporarily invaded by bacteria, it successfully withheld the attack of nature. Time has paused ever since.

Who on earth is she? Why did she have such an immortal body?

In ancient Egypt, people once successfully preserved the pharaohs' bodies in immortal mummies. However, the mummies were only dry shells. As regards the lifelike bodies in slough and wax, they were also reduced to empty shells. Before the discovery at Mawangdui, people had never discovered such a well-preserved wet body before. Later the bodies of the same kind have been referred to as "Mawangdui bodies".

To this day, people are still exploring unremittingly the secret of the immortality of the female body of Mawangdui. However, there is not a single explanation that can convince all.

Generally speaking, only under a very low temperature and in a non-oxygen environment can a wet body be preserved without decaying. Though the temperature of the ancient tomb remained stable, it cannot have been very low. Some guessed that perhaps the ancient people used some special method to keep the air from the tomb chamber.

The result of the excavation shows the unique structure of the tomb. The huge tomb chamber was placed at the bottom of the 20-meter-deep pit, surrounded by 0.5-meter-deep charcoals on each side. Outside the charcoals there is a layer of white paste mud that is 1 meter thick. Tampered earth and immature soil are then filled in the pit. Is the immortality of the body related to such a structure?

Obviously the charcoals are good at taking in water that has infiltrated the tomb. But what role does the white mud play?

Hou Liang
Former director of Mawangdui Excavation Team

Its formal name is crystalline kaolin. It is this that protected the body. It has a great density. The Geologic Bureau tested the mud and discovered that it did not leak after being immersed in water for 24 hours. It has such good waterproofing effects.

However, the same method used to be widely applied to the other tombs in South China, but did not achieve the same effect as at Mawangdui.

People suspect that there might be some unknown reasons for the immortality of the female body at Mawangdui. When it was unearthed, there was some mysterious liquid at the bottom of the inner coffin. From the result of the examination, the liquid contained ethanol and acetic acid, with a moderate acid pH scale of 5.18. Theoretically, such an environment is indeed helpful to prevent reproduction of bacteria. At that time the anatomy team for the female body specially distilled some of the liquid and did an experiment.

Liu Lihou
Professor of Xiangya Medical College of Mid-South University

The result showed that it had no effect at all. Judging from our experiment, this liquid has no preservative effect.

However, some also doubted the result. They held that since the liquid was not preserved well and that it was not the original liquid applied in the experiment, this could not prove anything. Since the clothes that wrapped the body were also immersed in the liquid, and these clothes included silk and hemp, their preservation was hard to explain.

Hou Liang
Former director of Mawangdui Excavation Team

For instance, silk is a kind of protein and is organic. It can stand acid. The liquid is an acid with a pH scale of 0. 05. However, the silk rotted away. Hemp is a plant fiber, which cannot stand acid, but it turned out to be very tough. I later took this hemp thread together with a new one to Beijing Paper-making Institute, and pulled them with a machine. The ancient thread snapped at about the same time as the new thread. So it can be said that this hemp thread functions as well as the new one. Now no physicists, biologists, or chemists can explain why the rules are violated here. So there are indeed many questions that remain unsolvable.

Where did the liquid come from and was it the liquid that caused the body to be preserved from decay? Some inferred that the liquid was a kind of preservative sprayed deliberately by ancient people before the burial; others think that it is a result of the congelation of the permeating vapor. Still others think that it is the water decomposed from the body.

Peng Longxiang
Professor of Xiangya Medical College of Mid-South University

That is to say, the human body is composed of 60 to 70 percent water. Originally the water was integrated in the body. When the body decays, the water decomposes and gathers into the water we have now.

No one can convince others with their different views. Many think that the female body of Mawangdui is only a historical coincidence and no similar delightful surprises will be likely to occur.

Over 20 years later, the miracle occurs once again. This time it is in Lianyungang, Jiangsu Province, which is 1000 kilometers far away from Changsha. In July, 2002, on a construction site of Shuanglong Village, people happened to discover a 5-meter-deep pit. The archaeologists inferred that this was a tomb where the husband and wife were buried together in the middle and later periods of the Western Han dynasty.

Three coffins were discovered. Among the three, the master, who enjoys the highest position, was intact in the skull and the encephalon was well preserved. However, the other two bodies had been almost completely rotted away.

There was only one coffin that was not opened on the spot and transported to Lianyungang Museum. The next morning, the archaeologists began clearing up coffin No. 3. When they were prying the lid with drills, they happened to break up a 5-cm-wide opening. Then something amazing happened. Through the opening, people clearly saw a foot.

After taking proper protective measures, at around 3 pm, the archaeologists opened the lid of the coffin, and an intact ancient body floating on her back in brown coffin liquid emerged in front of their eyes.

This discovery again brought hope to people. Perhaps her appearance can solve the mystery of the immortality of the mistress's body at Mawangdui.

In June, 2003, the female body in Lianyungang was sent to People's Hospital, where experts from Nanjing and Shanghai gathered together and studied the secret of the body. The medical staff carried out an all-around physical examination with X ray and CT scanning. The examination shows that the left eyeball of the body was relatively complete, and that her brain, though shrunk, was still very clear.

Han Qunying
Professor of Basic Medical College of Nanjing Medical University

Most of her skin is very fine and smooth. For example, the skin on her back is very good.

Later experts carried out an anatomy of the body. The result revealed even more astounding discoveries. Though having been shrunken to half of its original size,

The Part of the Outward Wrapping Silk on the Master's Body

The Lianyungang Tomb Buried in the Western Han Dynasty

her brain was well preserved, with the frontal gyri remaining very clear and the trigeminal preserved in good condition. The muscle, when pulled, still had elasticity and tenacity. Her spine was straight and the lines on her feet were clear. When her thorax and abdomen were opened, people could see that her viscera organs were complete. Though sticking to each other, such organs as the heart, the lungs, the liver and the intestines could still be differentiated.

The result of the anatomy is still in need of thorough analysis, from which we will get to know more about the anthropological and pathological implications. However, there was not an answer yet for the mystery of the immortality of the body.

Compared with the conditions of the Mawangdui tomb, that of the Lianyungang tomb was much simpler. It had relatively little mound, and there were not much charcoal and white pasty mud. What puzzled people most is that in the same tomb, under the same environment and the same airproof conditions, while there were only sporadic bones left in the other three coffins, why was only this female body so lucky?

The Legend of Mawangdui

The coffin liquid upon the discovery of the body attracted people's attention. This makes us associate it with the discovery of the coffin of the mistress at Mawangdui. However, according to the analysis of the liquid sample, the pH scale of the liquid was the slightly alkaline 7.55. It even contained hemoglobin. This is totally different from the acid liquid in the coffin of Mawangdui. Theoretically speaking, alkaline liquid not only cannot prevent the growth of bacteria, but can also help the reproduction of bacteria.

This was beyond people's expectations. The discovery of the female body at Lianyungang not only did not provide us with any clue to the mystery of the mistress of Mawangdui, but added new problems to it.

There may have been many coincidences contributing to the immortality of the body. However, researchers have tried their best to provide a passable answer. They attributed the immortality of the body to three reasons: the depth of the coffin, the airproof environment, and the lack of oxygen. Besides, it may also be related to the specific geographic conditions.

This time the archaeologists had better luck than in the case of Mawangdui. The unearthed relics have confirmed the identity of the female body in Lianyungang. Her husband may have been a local official with a high status, while she herself was a noblewoman named "Ling Huiping" conferred specially by the emperor.

The restored picture shows that Ling Huiping was a beautiful woman. According to the inference, she was 1.65 meters tall. Among the Chinese girls of that time, she was taller than average and was a real beauty. However, it is strange that such a beautiful and graceful marquise did not leave behind her many burial objects, which shows that her family was not very rich.

Compared with her, the mistress of Mawangdui, who belonged to the same rank of marquis of the Western Han dynasty, appeared to be affluent. Did this mistress enjoy an even higher status than the marquise? What are her countenance and character like? Is it possible for modern people to witness her beauty? Does her body hold the history of the vicissitudes of a great family?

As all other noblewomen, Xin Zhui paid great attention to her clothes. Among the over 100 clothes that have been unearthed, there were a complete set of silk clothes, embroidery, and tapis. Various robes, clothes, shoes, even gloves and socks—every personal effect is included. Some call this dark underground world the "ancient fashion show".

Xinzhui left numerous treasures that had become important historical relics for today's research. People were surprised

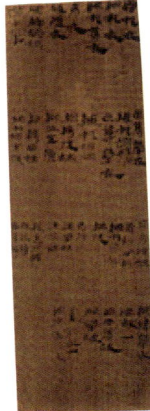

The Bamboo Slip with Chinese Characters

The Wooden Figurine

at the creations of humans from over 2000 years ago, especially at their expertise at silk making.

Bai Rongjin:
Expert of the Archaeological Institute of Chinese Academy of Social Sciences

That's why Mawangdu is an underground treasure house of ancient silk. Never in Chinese archaeological history have such a large number of well-preserved clothes.

A transparent zen robe weighs only 48 grams. Aside from the edges at the neckline and the cuffs, it weighs only 25 grams. It is said that when folded, it can be put into a normal-sized matchbox. Ancient Chinese described top-class silk clothes as being as thin as the wings of a cicada and as light as a flowing smoke. With this object at hand, archaeologists found out that such a description was no exaggeration at all.

Hou Liang
Former director of Mawangdui Excavation Team

This silk has a very fine quality. Look at the plain zen robe which weighs less than 1 tael. This shows that its silk is fine and has a high quality.

So our colleagues from Shanghai Textile Institute concluded that, from this robe we can see that back in the Han Dynasty, the techniques of planting mulberry trees, raising silkworms, and silk reeling and weaving were very advanced in the Changsha region. So till now we have not been able to produce a successful duplicate of the original. The replicate robe always exceeds 1 tael.

Xin Zhui also left many personal effects for women.

Though over 2000 years old, the unearthed cosmetic instruments are by no means inferior to those used by modern women. This lacquer case is the dressing case of Ms. Marquise. It is divided into two layers. On the top layer was placed a bronze mirror, and the layer below contains 9 small cases, where powder puffs, powder brushes, wooden combs and various cosmetics such as rouge and whitening powder were placed.

People discovered in the body that Xin Zhui was also wearing a pretty wig. The wig is in the shape of a knot, which was fixed on her own hair with 3 hairpins that differ in texture.

The greatest treasure of the Xin Zhui Tomb is perhaps the colorful lacquer wares. There are altogether over 700 pieces of lacquer wares, including dish wares, furniture, weapons, and gambling instruments for entertainment.

The lacquer wares are usually made of bamboo or wood. After such techniques as lacquering and painting, the lacquer wares will be painted with a transparent lacquer coat. The lacquer wares are light, practical, and enduring, which account for its general popularity in the Han Dynasty.

Zhou Shirong
Former vice director of Mawangdui Excavation Team

Han Dynasty was the golden age of lacquer wares. This fact can be best shown through Mawangdui.

A Transparent Zen Robe

This batch of lacquer wares in Mawangdui boasts the masterpieces of Han lacquer wares. They are peerless with the shiny luster, simple designs, varied cloud patterns, and bright colors.

Zhou Shirong:

In terms of colors and chromatics, there are the three primary colors of red, yellow and blue. However, there are many intermediary colors. In the blue family we have pinkish green, green, and dark green. There is a range of colors within it. The lacquer wares have many intermediary colors. There are also many varieties of the red color, including vermilion and mauve. So it can be inferred that the colors of Mawangdui lacquer wares are richer than those of the Period of the Warring States.

Due to the good airproof environment of the tomb, the lacquer wares, which should have been difficult to preserve, are preserved in good shape. Their colors and brightness stood the test of over 2000 years and look as if they were newly made. This even created a misunderstanding on the part of the foreign guests.

Hou Liang
Former director of Mawangdui Excavation Team

The guest saw a batch of shining lacquer wares and asked me, "Are they really relics from 2000 years ago?" I said yes. He asked, "Did you paint something on the outside?" He thought we had processed them by painting another coat of lacquer. I said no. I did not take it seriously and thought it was a casual question.

After the visit, He shook my hand and bid goodbye to me at the gate. He asked me again, "What did you paint on the lacquer wares?" I realized that he was serious and so I said that in China, the central government has a policy for cultural relic protection, which prescribes that every historical relic should be preserved in the original shape and any processing means damage to it and is a mistake to be punished. "Oh", He nodded. And then finally believed me.

A question came up about the burial objects. Why are there no bronze, gold or silver wares among the many luxuriant objects?

According to the historical record, at the beginning of the Western Han Dynasty, due to the weakness of the regime, several emperors have adopted the policy of rehabilitation. They promoted simplicity and a plain lifestyle. Emperor Wendi prescribed that the burial objects of the

The Dressing Case

noblemen should not include bronze wares or gold and silver jewelries.

On the surface, Xin Zhui did not violate the Emperor's stipulation. However, she did not follow the Emperor's word really. Everything shows that Xin Zhui is a greedy woman, since at that time, silk and lacquer wares were also luxuriant objects.

Zhou Shirong
Former vice director of Mawangdui Excavation Team

One lacquer ware is worth ten bronze ones. So although there is not any bronze ware in the tomb, the lacquer wares are even more expensive.

The luxury of the tomb leads us to the imagination of the mistress' spectacular palace before her death. She must have had hundreds and thousands of servants, innumerous treasures and delicate food.

What is the mysterious Xin Zhui like? How eminent was her family? If she is not the wife of Marquis Dai, who is she?

When Tomb No.1 was under excavation, there was a saying in Changsha that in the two mounds of Mawangdui were buried two imperial concubines of Emperor Jingdi of the Western Han Dynasty. This saying is also consistent with the chorography. As to the objects from Marquis Dai, they might have been tributes to the imperial concubine.

Before the confirmation of the mistress' identity, even archaeologists were tempted by this thought. The luxuriant burial objects are in accordance with the status of an imperial concubine.

The two mounds of Mawangdui looked indeed like the mounds of two tombs. This indicates that there is a Tomb No.2 to the east of Xin Zhui's Tomb. Are they really the tombs of the two imperial concubines?

However, in the course of the excavation of Xin Zhui's Tomb, it was discovered that strange gas similar to that of Tomb

The Lacquer Cosmetic Case

The Small Cases in the Lacquer Cosmetic Case

No.1 surprisingly came out from the south. Probably there was a third tomb to the south.

Hou Liang
Former director of Mawangdui Excavation Team

I sent an official together with a member of our team to explore whether this was a tomb or not. However, a member of our team was so rash that he hoed a hole in the ground.

As a result, the charcoal inside flowed out immediately. He had a look inside. Alas, There was another big coffin. The big coffin of Tomb No.3 emerged. "This is indeed a big tomb", he said. Only then did we know there were 3 tombs here.

Tombs No. 1 and 2 are arranged from east to west and Tomb No. 3 is close to Tomb No. 1 to the south. Since Tomb No. 3 has been exposed, archaeologists decided to excavate it first.

In November 1973, Mawangdui was busy and crowded once again.

Chinese Archaeological Discoveries

The Lacquer Wares

This time people were more expectant than doubtful. Everyone hoped to come across delightful surprises in this tomb. Better equipped this time, they could better protect the bodies and carry out more thorough research on them. The clues to the identity of Xin Zhui of Tomb No. 1 and the mystery of her immortality might be found at Tomb No. 3.

However, an accident occurred when the archaeological team came to the southeastern corner of the tomb.

Hou Liang
Former director of Mawangdui Excavation Team

At this corner, there was a strip that, about 30 to 40 cm wide and over 1 meter long. In this strip there were only charcoals without white pasty mud. In other places, the white mud was thick on top and thin below, But here there was no white mud at all.

The team was very concerned. No matter the reason, the absence of white pasty mud might undermine the protection of the tomb. The spectacular scene at Tomb No.1 might not repeat itself here. The result of the excavation testified to people's concerns. Due to the lack of an enclosed environment, Tomb No. 3 suffered from a serious leakage of water.

Compared with that of Tomb No.1, the scale of Tomb No.3 was relatively small. The coffin was divided into 3 layers, with the wing rooms filled with abundant burial objects. Later many of them were confirmed to be rare treasures. However, the condition of the inner coffin was disappointing. The researchers attempted to extract the coffin liquid with the prepared vacuum pump, but it turned out to be in vain.

Fu Juyou
Former vice curator of Hunan Museum

When we drilled with the vacuum pump, we saw that the coffin had split. It was leaking. So we didn't need to extract the liquid.

The master of Tomb No. 3 was reduced to a skeleton. Medical experts examined him and inferred that he was a young man in his early thirties. The mystery of the immortality of the female body was not solved at Tomb No. 3, and the hypothesis that the mistresses of the tombs were two imperial concubines was not supported either.

Though the master of Tomb No.3 did not bring to the posterity the wonder of immortality, he left with us another precious treasure.

Many books copied on silk and bamboo slips were discovered here. They documented a wide range of content, which reflected the outstanding wisdom and profound culture of the Chinese people. The 120,000-word silk books included the famous ancient classics of *Book of Changes* and *Laozi*, etc. Most of them are ancient classics that have been lost for one to two thousand years.

This is the largest discovery of ancient classics since the discovery of Dunhuang. Later even an independent discipline was formed of the studies on the books on silk and bamboo slips at Mawangdui, called Mawangdui Studies.

Hou Liang
Former director of Mawangdui Excavation Team

Why are these books on silk so precious? Because there are many books that were not even recorded by Sima Qian in his *Shi Ji* (Historical Records) and preserved here. The lost books have been rediscovered. Another reason is that these versions of the classics are very old. Take *Dao De Jing* for example, we talk about *Dao De Jing* and about *Laozi* all the time. However, here is *De Dao Jing*, that is, the De text

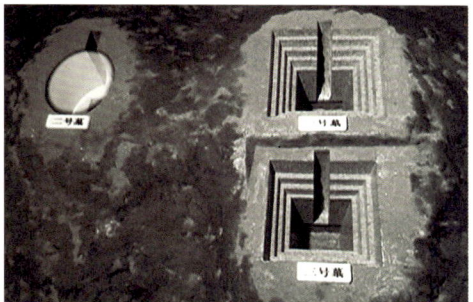

The Position of the Three Tombs

proceeds the Dao one. Similarly there are many other mistakes in the popular versions of the classics that have been corrected in these books.

There was also a painting on silk at Tomb No. 3, in which the people were making various gestures. Some were spreading their arms like birds, others are crawling clumsily upward like bears. There are altogether 40 movements, with running commentaries in the margin. This is the physical exercise of the time and the primitive ancestor of shadowboxing.

The prowess of the ancient Chinese in astronomy is also amazing. The picture of a comet gives such an accurate report of the image and position of the comets, which almost makes people doubt whether it was really the result of naked-eye observation.

The over-6000-word *Wu Xing Zhan*, which means the astrology of the five major stars not only records down the astrology of ancient Chinese, but also their understanding of the universe.

Mercury, Venus, Mars, Jupiter, and Saturn are the five major planets of the solar system observable to the naked eye. *Wu Xing Zhan* left some data observed with the naked eye, which reflects the relatively accurate understanding of the law of movement of the five major planets of the ancient people.

Fu Juyou
Former vice curator of Hunan Museum

The cycles of the revolution and meeting of the five major planets of the solar system—compared with the data we have now—are recorded as over 580 days, which deviates only half a day from the accurate data. Such accuracy had never been achieved in world astronomical history in any other country.

In the tomb there was a Relief Map. The map was drawn from south to north vertically and is to scale. The map records the geographical conditions from E 111° to E 112°30'in longitude and from N 23° to N 26°in latitude. It roughly includes the border region between Hunan, Guangdong and Guangxi, which stretches to today's Kowloon and Hong Kong. This 2000-year-old map has the four major elements of a modern map, namely, mountains, rivers, roads and residential areas.

Fu Juyou:

With the four major elements, the map is very scientific indeed. It is in rough accordance with the modern map in the depiction of the direction of the river and its curving shape. If we compare

The Excavation Spot of Tomb No.3

this map with modern sailing maps it may fall short. But compared with maps of the Qing Dynasty, it is more accurate.

Judging from the burial objects, the master of Tomb No. 3 was an erudite person. He was well educated and enjoyed reading very much.

However, he is not a gentle and weak bookworm, since many weapons were also unearthed. People inferred that the master of Tomb No. 3 might have been a military officer of Changsha State.

Two paintings on silk were discovered at Tomb No. 3, and the man on the painting must be the master of the tomb.

Why did such a young and vigorous officer die at the prime age of 30? Did he die from a sudden attack of a serious

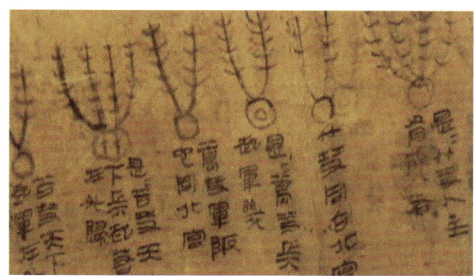
The Picture of a Comet

illness? Is there another complicated story involved?

History shows that at the beginning of the Western Han Dynasty, the southern Nan Yue State rebelled. Changsha State was the frontier in this battle against the rebellions. The troops between the two states had an arduous battle. Due to the abominable natural conditions of the battlefield, both parties suffered a substantial loss.

Therefore, it is inferred that the master of Tomb No.3 led his army in the battle against the rebellious troops and unfortunately died in the battle. His body was carried back to Changsha and buried in a haste.

Then, who is he and what relation does he have to Xin Zhui, the mistress of Tomb No.1? There were no clear clues to the identity of the master. People began to place hope on Tomb No.2.

Tomb No. 2 is only 23 meters from the western wall of Tomb No.1. Starting from December, 1973, archaeologists carried out excavations of Tomb No.2.

Fu Juyou
Former vice curator of Hunan Museum

When we excavated Tomb No.2, we were full of hopes and expectations of it. At that time the mound was huge. It was as big as that of Tomb No.1. We followed the archaeological method by probing for the stratum structure first. We did not dig the mound immediately, but removed half of it like slicing a bread. From this section plane we could detect the stratum structure, that is, the stratums' chronological order. So we invited a mechanical construction company and pulled half of the mound with a bulldozer. After that, we found the tomb entrance was in the shape of an ellipse.

The elliptical entrance puzzled everyone on the spot. Why do the two tombs in the same tomb complex have different entrances?

Fu Juyou:

An expert from the Archaeological Institute said that it was not a tomb. He said that among so many Han tombs throughout China among the tens of thousands of tombs that had been excavated, there was not a single tomb with an elliptical entrance. Never.

The archaeologists on the spot had a heated discussion. Some thought that this might not be a tomb, but the result of the collapse of the surface stratum. They decided to have the ground probed with a bore.

Chinese Archaeological Discoveries

The *Book of Changes* on Silk

Fu Juyou
Former vice curator of Hunan Museum

The drill went down 10 meters in 2 or 3 hours. The aiguille was so big that it even struck down the white pasty mud. That was indeed a tomb.

Although the entrance was not regular, it must be a tomb. What might this tomb leave us? Soon after the excavations, several holes by tomb plunderers were discovered successively.

Fu Juyou:
There were so many holes in the tomb, that we were truly disappointed.

In one of the holes, a porcelain bowl of the Tang Dynasty was accidentally discovered. This indicates that as early as the Tang Dynasty, Tomb No. 2 was visited by tomb plunderers.

Fu Juyou:
The coffin had rotted away and was reduced to the bottom plank. There was nothing but mud and water all mingling together. So we stopped drilling for the time, since we had to clear up the relics.

Hou Liang
Former director of Mawangdui Excavation Team

The leaked water put pressure on the coffin

A Relief Map

and had broken it. So the planks on the side were all rotted away. The lid fell down onto the bottom. There were not many relics in the tomb — altogether over 400 relics — and were all destroyed.

The scale of Tomb No.2 is obviously much smaller than those of Tombs No.1 and No.3. The burial objects also appeared to be humbler. If the mistresses of Tomb No.1 and 2 were both imperial concubines as rumored, why is there such a great gap?

It was severe winter then. A great snow suddenly came to Changsha.

Zhou Shirong
Former vice director of Mawangdui Excavation Team

It was freezing cold and soon to be Spring Festival. It seemed there was hardly anything left at the tomb. In the freezing weather, how were we going to proceed with the excavation?

Fu Juyou
Former vice curator of Hunan Museum

I said it not only can be cleared up but should be quickly cleared up. There was no time to waste. Now it was snowing and the water was frozen. We should use this time to clear up the tomb. If we waited until the tomb gets oxygenized with the ice and water, it might collapse. So I said 'hurry up'.

Due to the destruction of the tomb chamber, the burial objects were scattered about in a mess. The archaeologists had to grope in mud and water. Suddenly, someone picked up two seals from the mud.

The Painting on Silk in Tomb No.3

Gao Zhixi

Former curator of Hunan Museum

We discovered at the tomb two seals. One was inscribed "Li Cang" and "Marquis Dai's Seal" and the other was inscribed "Li Cang's Jade Seal". Well, we were very happy then. I said, finally we can determine the identity of the master.

Judging from the seals, the master of Tomb No.2 is Marquis Dai with the name of Li Cang. The inscriptions of Marquis Dai showed up many times in the burial objects of Tombs No.1 and 2.

Marquis Dai, or Li Cang used to be the Prime Minister of Changsha State at the beginning of the Western Han Dynasty. If the identity of the master is confirmed, then there should be a seal inscribed "Prime Minister of Changsha State".

Gao Zhixi:

We decided that after clearing up the relics, we

Marquis Dai's Seal

should hoist the bottom planks of the coffin and carry back the mud under them to our museum.

Zhou Shirong
Former vice director of Mawangdui Excavation Team

I drew the marks. I drew the number 1 here, and placed basket number 1 here. And I drew the number 2 there and placed basket number 2 there. So we took the baskets back and cleared them up one by one. Alas, there it was.

Gao Zhixi
Former curator of Hunan Museum

There was nothing but this seal in more than one load of mud. We only found this seal.

This seal supported people's inference. The inscription clearly shows "Prime Minister of Changsha".

Zhou Shirong:

So the greatest value in Tomb Number 2 lies in the three seals.

The discovery of the three seals have become the greatest contribution of Tomb No.2. The identities of the three masters of

Li Cang's Seal

The Seal of Prime Minister of Changsha State

the tombs have finally been clarified. All the hypotheses have stopped ever since. The master of Tomb No.2 is Li Cang, the mistress of Tomb No.1 is undoubtedly the wife of Li Cang, the Marquise, and the master of Tomb No. 3 should have been Li Cang's son.

Hou Liang
Former director of Mawangdui Excavation Team

Well, the mystery has finally been settled. Comrade Wang Xu from Beijing said, "Well, we have found the eyes of Mawangdui."

Though the identities of the tomb masters have been settled, this has further aroused people's questions.

How can a family of a minor marquis possessing 700 households come to be as wealthy as the imperial family? At the beginning of Western Han Dynasty, Changsha region was relatively poor. Besides the tributes of the feudatory, what financial resources did this family have?

Furthermore, why was Xin Zhui's tomb so much more exquisite than her husband's?

The advanced historical records in ancient China further enriched the information about the Marquis Dai family. In 193 BC, Li Cang, Prime Minister of Changsha State was conferred by Emperor Wendi as Marquis Dai. Eight years later, Li Cang died. The narrow pit and simple burial objects of Li Cang's Tomb show that at that time he was not very rich. The elliptical entrance might also be due to the lack of money.

After Li Cang's death, his son Li Xi inherited his title and became the second Marquis Dai.

Is this Marquis Dai the master of Tomb No.3 that died in the war? In the ensuing archaeological researches, people had a heated discussion over the identity of the master of Tomb No.3. Some experts think that he is indeed Li Xi, the second Marquis Dai, whereas others questioned this opinion, for the coffin in Tomb No.3 is divided into 3 layers, which violates the burial institutions appropriate for a marquis. So he should not be Li Xi, the second Marquis Dai. Furthermore, the arrangement of Tombs No.3 and 1 does not accord with this hypothesis.

People inferred that Li Cang might have another son.

The Seal of Prime Minister of Changsha State

Gao Zhixi
Former curator of Hunan Museum

If Tomb Number 3 indeed belonged to Li Xi, he could not have been buried at his mother's feet. He was, after all, a marquis, and how can a marquis be buried at his mother's feet? So the inference that the smaller son was buried here is very reasonable.

If the master of Tomb No.3 is not Li Xi, the second Marquis Dai, then where should his tomb be? In this family tomb complex where three masters are buried, should there be a fourth tomb? Experts decided to have the drilling workers carry out another close probing to the two mounds.

Fu Juyou
Former vice curator of Hunan Museum

The drilling team worked for three days and explored everywhere. They found nothing.

The experts who thought that Tomb No.3 belonged to Li Xi were further convinced in their judgment. They also found the related evidence in the burial objects of Tomb No.3. In some lutes of Tomb No.3, there clearly left the four characters of "Chamberlain of Marquis Dai". In the social institution of Han Dynasty, only feudal princes are entitled to having chamberlains. The rank equals the head of a county.

On the lacquer wares there are many inscriptions indicating the owners' identities. "Wine for Your Majesty", and "Food for Your Majesty". One has to be

The Lutes with the Four Characters of "Chamberlain of Marquis Dai"

at least a feudal prince to be called "Your Majesty". Besides, the unearthed paintings on silk depicted the master's cart to be a four-horse one.

Fu Juyou:

The emperor can have a 6-horse cart, feudal princes 4-horse ones, the ministers 3-horse ones and the inferior noblemen 2-horse ones. Common people can only have 1-horse carts. If you want to drive a 4-horse cart, you trespass the institution and violate the law.

For many years, similar controversy has been going on and on. The Han Tombs of Mawangdui remain mysterious and tempting. Some of the problems may be solved in the future, while others may not.

Modern people are more interested in Xin Zhui, the immortal mistress of Tomb No.1. The historical records have completely neglected her, but over 2000 years later, she attracts much more attention than her husband and son.

The Lacquer Ware with the Inscription of "Food for Your Majesty"

In March, 2002, at the invitation of Hunan Museum, Prof. Zhao Chengwen of the Legal Medical Physician Department of China Police College began to restore the image of Xin Zhui. For the convenience of police work, Prof. Zhao designed a software called CCK-3 human image simulation system, which can restore a dead person's face from the skull. Prof. Zhao thinks that the key to a person's face lies in the shape of the skull. As long as the skull is complete, the female body of over 2000 years ago is basically no different than the body discovered in a modern criminal case.

The restoration is mainly based on the X-ray of Xin Zhui's skull, the photos of her face when unearthed, the paintings on the silk, and the related historical literature. Prof. Zhao completed the restoration of Xin Zhui's face in his computer.

She seems to be a real Chinese beauty.

From the length of the body, it can be inferred that she was about 1.6 meters tall when she was young. On the basis of this, people replicated a waxwork of the youthful Xin Zhui.

No records show the origin of Xin Zhui. People inferred that when very young, this beauty had been married to Li Cang, who was much older than her.

At her husband's death, Xin Zhui was only in her thirties and was not well-off. Later, Li Cang's son, Li Xi, inherited the title of marquis, and the family remained in Changsha.

No one can depict for sure the story of Xin Zhui. What pains did she have? What puzzles did she encounter? Perhaps she was even involved in some romantic affairs. How did such a beautiful widow manage the family?

After Li Cang's death, the family of Marquis Dai did not decline but boomed. By what means did Xin Zhui accumulate such great wealth? Perhaps she threw herself into the lap of certain personages, and perhaps she used some special means to become rich. However, the answer has long sunk into the depth of history, and we can only rely on our imagination to depict Xin Zhui's life.

She might have been happy. She indulged herself in the beautiful clothes and delicate food and knew no constraints in the family. When old age approached her, she was full of fear. So she placed all her consolation on her after-death palace, and had many workers build up another luxuriant residence and spent money like water in ordering expensive lacquer wares and silk textiles.

In the course of the excavation, people were puzzled with the painting on silk covering the lid of the innermost coffin. For a long time afterwards, this painting has always had a unique charm. It attracts people's attention, for it is not only a beautiful artistic piece, but also reveals the secret in Xin Zhui's heart and the ancient Chinese understanding of the universe, as well as life and death.

The painting is more than 2 meters long. It is divided into three parts, the lower part hell, the middle part the human world, and the upper part the heaven.

Hell does not look very scary, with a barebacked man standing on the top of a strange fish and supporting the ground with his head and hands.

The human world is a depiction of Xin Zhui's life. She is an elegant old woman surrounded by servants. Her facial expression was serene and somewhat melancholy.

With the appropriate proportion, the

The Waxwork of Xin Zhui

smooth strokes, and the vivid figures, the portrait is a masterpiece in traditional Chinese portrait painting.

The heaven that Xin Zhui longed for is depicted as such: there are 9 strange suns shining between huge bows. In the middle of the biggest sun there stands a golden crow. In the crescent there are the legendary celestial rabbit and toad, with a dancing fairy beside them. The figures in the center at the top of the painting must be the goddess. She has the body of a snake and is the creator in Chinese legends—Nü Wa.

People inferred that this painting was in fact a flag, which calls for the soul of the dead. Perhaps Xin Zhui was not sure she

The Legend of Mawangdui

The T-shaped Silk Painting Divided into Three Parts

of her after-death world, while she did not anticipate the vicissitudes of her family in the future.

According to the history, after Li Xi's death, his son, the third Marquis Dai left Changsha and became an official in the capital city of Chang'an. Later, the fourth Marquis Dai was also a military officer but was sentenced to death for moving forces without acquiring permission. He escaped the death penalty only by amnesty and had to come back to his hometown.

The records of Marquis Dai family has stopped there. Only several decades after Xin Zhui's death, the once wealthy and dignified family was no more, her posterity became common people and the past riches and honor dissipated like clouds.

Marquise Xin Zhui left the world with many precious relics and unsolvable mysteries; however, her own wishes and aspirations have irretrievably faded away into the ashes of history.

could be elevated to heaven, so she had this exquisite flag made to guide her soul lest she took the wrong way.

Xin Zhui concentrated in the construction

Ancient Wine Workshop

Over 3000 years ago, the ancient Chinese innovated a material called "distiller's yeast". Liquor brewed with such an ingredient is luscious, fragrant, carries a lingering aftertaste. For thousands of years, distiller's yeast has been the key to the brewage of Chinese liquor, and the history of liquor brewage and appreciation has long been a unique cultural phenomenon in China. However, not many Chinese understand how their ancestors used to brew good liquor, nor how many legends and anecdotes have been buried in the depths of history.

Chengdu, the capital city of Sichuan, was the capital of the ancient state of Shu about 2500 years ago. For over 2000 years, it has been one of the most affluent and prosperous cities in Southwestern China.

There are two ancient artificial rivers in the downtown areas of Chengdu, namely, Fuhe River and Nanhe River. They are part of the well-known ancient irrigation works of Dujiangyan. At the jointure of the two rivers, an elegant pavilion was specially built. Its name is "Hejiang Pavilion", which means literally "River Jointure Pavilion".

Near the Hejiang Pavilion lies an ancient lane called "Shuijing Street", which means "Well Street". This small, unnoticed lane is no more than 5 Chinese li long and 5 meters wide.

At the end of the 20th century, an incident made Shuijing Street instantly famous around China.

The story begins with this common courtyard.

No. 19, Shuijing Street. At the gate a dense fragrance of liquor was in the air. Inside the courtyard there is in fact the brewing workshop of a wine factory.

Mr. Cui Tiquan is 87 years old now. He began his apprenticeship at the wine factory in his early youth. Later he became the well-known experienced brewer of the factory, the "brewing master" by the jargon of this trade, and many stories about the brewery industry of Shuijing Street have remained in this old man's memory.

Cui Tiquan

Senior worker of the Wine Workshop

The good quality of the liquor produced at this workshop of Shuijing Street is mainly due to the old wine cellar. The cellar of Shuijing Workshop enjoys an enduring reputation and a proud history of at least 500 to 600 years.

Ancient Wine Workshop

The recorded history of No. 19, Shuijing Street starts from this old contract. The year when the contract went into effect was the 4th year during Emperor Daoguang's reign of the Qing Dynasty, which is 1824 AD. The factory was then a wine workshop in this courtyard called "Quan Xing Cheng". In this light, the history of this ancient wine workshop is at best 200 years long. Is the history of "five to six hundred years" just the tall tale of the senior folks?

In August 1998, the wine factory was going to have its compounding workshop expanded and repaired. It came to Mr. Cui Tiquan and other experienced workers' mind that a treasure was said to have been buried underground. If the saying was true, the treasure might well be destroyed by the construction. The advice of the senior workers was accepted and a tentative exploration was made beforehand. To everyone's amazement, something did emerge from the ground.

Li Wenhua

Official of the Office for the Protection of the Site of Shuijing Workshop

We dug out many ceramic fragments. Judging from the characters of the fragments, we inferred that they might belong to the Ming Dynasty. This attracted high attention from leaders of the factory and they reported the discovery immediately to the concerned governmental departments. Archaeologists were also invited to the spot.

The archaeologists held that there might be ancient relics of high historical value beneath the wine factory of Shuijing Street. After heated discussions for quite some time, the factory gave up the expansion plan. In March 1999, an archaeological team entered the spot and began the excavations.

No.19 of Shuijing Street in Chengdu

Chen Jian

Associate research fellow of Archaeological Institute of Chengdu, Sichuan Province, and leader of the excavation of the site of Shuijing Workshop

At the time of the excavation, this factory was still in operation, which poses some difficulties to our work. However, we soon discovered a site of a Qing Dynasty wine workshop beneath the factory. Quite unexpectedly, further excavations revealed another wine workshop of the Ming Dynasty, which is beneath the Qing one.

The initial discovery proves the senior folks' story to be true. This is indeed a historical site of a wine workshop, on which there are three successive layers of history. On top lies the workshop of the modern and contemporary times, which is still in operation today. The layer below is the ancient site of a wine workshop of the Qing Dynasty, which was further built on an ancient wine workshop that dates back to the Ming times and before.

A month later, the archaeologists had made a tentative conclusion that the site covered an area of about 1,700 square meters. Since the factory was still in operation, the area available for excavation was limited. Only 280 square meters actually received excavations. However, the ancient relics excavated from such a small area had become a hot topic for the media and the public.

The ancient wine workshop attracted many people's interest. Wine has become an indispensable part of modern life. But when did people begin to drink wine? What kind of wine did our ancestors drink? How was wine brewed in the past?

It is said that Chinese learned brewing techniques since six or seven thousand years ago. In the Erlitou cultural site of Henan Province, archaeologists discovered for the first time the earliest bronze wine vessels in China.

The advanced agricultural civilization provided ancient Chinese with abundant food. From the very beginning, Chinese people have adopted food as the major material of liquor brewage. Guided with their expertise and instinct, they have mastered the technique of distiller's yeast production as early as 3000 years ago, which is their great contribution to brewing technology.

This brick-like stuff is distiller's yeast. It is mainly composed of starch. With the yeast, various mildews can be grown, which can in turn produce a large amount of amylase, serving as the catalyst to the process of food sweetening and fermentation.

However, modern people had been

Ancient Wine Workshop

The Distiller's Yeast

The Cooking Range Site

limited to the related records of ancient literature as regards the actual brewage process of ancient Chinese, since no material objects had been available. The excavation of the Shuijing Workshop has for the first time enabled people to see the whole brewage process of the ancient Chinese.

Here is the cooking range site. There are altogether four such cooking ranges, among which two are modern ones and the other two are ones of the Qing Dynasty.

The steaming and boiling of food is the first procedure of Chinese brewage. Mingled with the distiller's yeast and steamed and boiled, food is easier to be fermented.

Traditionally, the half wrought food should be sprayed on the ground once out of the boiler. This consists of the second procedure, namely, the churning, ingredient mixing, piling and initial fermentation. There is a special name for the ground where the food is dried and basked, that is the "air hall".

These flat grounds excavated from the site of Shuijing Workshop are the air halls. There are altogether three such halls built one upon another that have been excavated from the site, which were constructed with caesious square bricks and tabia (the air halls of the Qing Dynasty had a rough surface, whereas the muddy air halls of the

The Wine Workshop

89

The Site of "Air Hall"

earlier Yuan and Ming dynasties were very smooth. Experts analyzed that this was because the drying instruments of the Qing Dynasty were harder.)

These earth pits beside the air halls are the sites of wine cellars. They look like huge wine jars stuck underground. 8 wine cellars were excavated from Shuijing Workshop, whose interior walls and bottoms were daubed with pure yellow mud. The thickness of the mud layer varies from 8 to 25 centimeters.

Here in the cellars the third procedure is carried out—the further fermentation of materials. The muddy walls buried underground for hundreds of years used to be immersed with the semi-finished alcohol for a long time and still gives out dense mellow fragrances and alluring luster.

The fermented alcohol in the wine cellars is still low in alcohol density. To acquire a higher alcohol density, it needs further distillation and condensation. Traditionally, this step is carried out with the vaporizer, the so-called "heavenly boiler".

However, at the beginning, people did not find relics of the "heavenly boilers". Isn't this the workshop of distilled liquor?

For a long time, Chinese drank brewed liquor, liquor without the procedure of distillation. This kind of liquor has a relatively low alcohol content.

The story of Wu Song's killing a tiger is famous in China. Despite the shop owner's warning, Wu Song drank 18 bowls of liquor before climbing the Jingyang Hill. He killed a tiger there while deeply drunk.

Among the alcohols produced in all parts of China, those with 38 degrees of alcohol density are regarded as "light" alcohols. Normally the so-called "rack" has an alcohol density ranging from 40 to 60 degrees. According to this standard, 1000 years ago, Wu Song drank at least 2 kilograms of liquor, which is equal to 4 standard bottles of liquor. Having drunk so much alcohol, one would have had difficulties in taking a step. No one believes such a capacity for liquor. Therefore, some believe that the liquor Wu Song drank then was not what we call "rack" today, but light unfiltered wine such as yellow wine.

Today, brewed wine such as yellow wine receives as much popularity as the distilled ones. The biggest difference between the two types of liquor in terms of manufacturing technique is the presence of distillation in the production of the latter.

What did the Shuijing Street workshop produce, brewed yellow wine or distilled liquor? The key to the question lies in whether vaporizers can be found or not. Are there any vaporizers hidden in this ancient workshop?

Archaeologists discovered then on the layer of the Qing Dynasty this strange-looking round relic. On first sight, it resembles a well.

Chen Jian
Associate research fellow of Archaeological Institute of Chengdu, Sichuan Province, and leader of the excavation of the site of Shuijing Workshop

We anatomized its interior and did not discover regular well walls going underground.

It was constructed on the ground.

Then is it a grind or a base of a roller?

Chen Jian:
No, because it only made use of some stone slabs at the bottom of both sides of the grind, on the top of which there are some other related facilities. It is not useful in processing food.

Archaeologists drew the conclusion at last that this is the earliest confirmed material object for wine distillation in China. In the past, huge vaporizers were put up on the base. The vaporizers are divided into two layers, with the lower layer containing the wine for distillation, and the upper one containing cool water. Heated with the exuberant fire in the base, the wine is steamed and boiled, and the alcoholic steam is cooled off with the water above, condenses into liquid and flows out of the tube, creating distilled liquor.

People inferred that in the Qing Dynasty,

this workshop produced distilled liquor with very similar techniques to those of modern times.

Then was it also distilled liquor that was produced by this workshop in the earlier Ming Dynasty? The material used for distilled liquor in China is mostly broomcorn; however, no traces of broomcorn were found at the Shuijing Street site. One piece of evidence that the experts discovered from the mud in the wine cellars of the Ming Dynasty clarified people's doubts.

Zhuang Mingyang

Research fellow of the Biological Institute of Chinese Academy of Natural Sciences of Chengdu

We carried out tests with modern technology on the microbes of the ancient wine cellars of Shuijing Workshop. In particular, we separated red yeast and rhizopus. The liquor brewed with this proper mixture of microbes can only be produced from pot ale with distillation.

The Site of Wine Cellars

The archaeological work at Shuijing Workshop proves that by the end of the Yuan Dynasty and the beginning of Ming times, China possessed mature techniques for brewing distilled liquor. This discovery partly solved some doubts about the history of Chinese distilled liquor.

The history of distilled liquor in the world can be traced back to the 12th century AD. However, there had been controversy concerning the origin of distilled liquor in China. According to the records of *Compendium of Material Medical*, Chinese distilled liquor originated from the Yuan Dynasty, which was introduced by the Western Regions into the central plains.

The prestigious British scholar Dr. Joseph Needham did not agree with Li Shizhen's record. He thought that given the fact that Chinese had had the custom of steaming and boiling food since the Neolithic times, and that the vaporizer was easy to manufacture and had existed for a long time in China, it was hard to believe that such facilities were introduced from outside.

The modern archaeological discovery provided certain proof for Dr. Joseph Needham's idea. On the painted bricks of

Ancient Wine Workshop

The Earliest Material Object for Wine Distillation in China

the Han Dynasty unearthed in Sichuan were painted clearly the life and manufacturing methods related to wine in that period. This one, in particular, demonstrates the brewing method at that time. Some say that the manufacturing equipment was the vaporizer. However, some experts did not support this hypothesis.

Lin Xiang

Professor of the Archaeological Department of Sichuan University

　Obviously this is an instance of a "shop in front and workshop in the backyard". The backyard is for brewing wine, where wine is brewed with other ingredients in the wine jars. The front serves as the counter, below which there are many pots. There is a vehicle beside the counter to carry away all the wine. So it is not the vaporizer.

　This bronze ware from the Eastern Han Dynasty, collected at the Shanghai Museum, used to be regarded as the earliest vaporizer that had been discovered in China. The staff of the Museum even made a successful experiment with it by imitating the techniques for manufacturing distilled liquor.

　However, some experts had different opinions as regards the real use of this bronze utensil.

The Painted Bricks of the Han Dynasty

Lin Xiang
Professor of the Archaeological Department of Sichuan University

At that time this utensil was without a lid. During the experiment the staff added a lid to it, for we all knew that to distill the liquor we need an enclosed environment with a condenser on the top. Without a condenser, the steam is impossible to liquidize into alcohol. Since this utensil is without a lid, this fact aroused my doubt. The utensil is more probably used for the distillation of medicine and toilet water than for the distillation of wine.

Up to now, the archaeological excavations can only prove that at least by the Song Dynasty, Chinese had invented vaporizers in the modern sense, and that distilled liquor with a high density might have been produced in certain places.

Lin Xiang:

It can be safely concluded that the technique of distilling liquor in China probably originates in China. In the Yuan Dynasty, certain distillation techniques which enhanced our own were introduced from Central Asia.

Although the archaeological discovery at Shuijing Workshop did not solve the problem of the origin of China's vaporizers, it did provide the earliest material evidence for the distillation technique in China.

The Probable Earliest Vaporizer in China

Through hundreds of years of development, China's distillation techniques have matured with their own characteristics in fermentation and distillation methods. Chinese liquor, French brandy, Russian Vodka, and Scottish Whisky are regarded as the four major distilled liquors in the world. Chinese alcohol is the unique invention and precious treasure of the ancient Chinese civilization. Chinese distilled liquor is divided into dense fragrance, delicate fragrance, mellow fragrance and other types. The mellow fragrance liquor is smooth, the dense fragrance pure, and the delicate fragrance sweet and refreshing. All the varieties bring to people great enjoyment.

The liquor brewed at Shuijing Workshop belongs to the dense fragrance type. It is a variety of Chinese distilled alcohol that enjoys the widest distribution. Its distinguishing characteristics is that it is brewed in muddy cellars.

However, why should the wine cellar be built underground? From the technical perspective, it is more difficult and resource-consuming to build underground cellars for liquor brewage.

The Bamboo Slices Inserted in the Wine Cellar to Protect the Mud of the Cellar

Duan Yu

Research fellow of the Historical Institute of Sichuan Academy of Social Sciences

The wine cellars in Sichuan took the form of underground earth pits. According to our analyses, this fact is related to the alcohol prohibition of ancient times. China has a long history of alcohol prohibition. The Shang Dynasty was said to perish because of the Emperor's indulgence in alcohol. So at the time of the establishment of the Zhou Dynasty, the Emperor made a decision that no one, even the ministers at the court, should drink liquor, as it leads to national perdition. So alcohol prohibition was carried out in the ensuing dynasties as well, that is to say, nobody was allowed to drink liquor. However, it can be exclusively sold by the government.

Due to the chaos created by war in the north, many people fled to Sichuan, which was geographically detached from the outside. Since the central government was too far away to control the purchase of liquor, it was secretly produced in underground cellars in Sichuan. So the underground cellars are great characteristics of Sichuan liquor production.

What is more important, this expediency has become a special kind of technique in China's repertoire of liquor brewage.

Lin Xiang
Professor of the Archaeological Department of Sichuan University

Except the discovery at Shuijing Workshop in Sichuan Basin, the fermentation has until now been carried out in pottery jars or other pottery wares in China. The muddy cellars for corn fermentation originated from Chengdu Plain and Sichuan Basin. It is only in that place.

The oldest of these muddy cellars discovered at Shuijing Workshop has a history of nearly 600 years. This wine cellar is very special with many bamboo slices inserted in it. Experts inferred that they are used to protect the mud. It is said that the mud used in these cellars is specially taken from Phoenix Hill near Chengdu. The yellow mud on Phoenix

Hill is very lustrous and glutinous. All the experienced brewers remember the ancient idea of "treasuring the mud as gold and cherishing the cellar as life". Whenever the mud in the cellar is damaged a bit, workers would immediately mend it.

Why did the people pay such attention to the mud?

Lin Xiang
Professor of the Archaeological Department of Sichuan University

The microbe families in the soil participate in the fermentation and alcoholization, and combine the sweetening process with the alcoholization.

The mucor, rhizopus, and yeast form symbiosis in the earth with the various bacteria and alcoholize the grain into wine.

So the wine has an especially strong fragrance. Its fragrance far exceeds that of wine fermented with pottery jars. The strong fragrant wine forms another variety of Chinese liquor—mellow fragrance liquor, all of which is fermented with mud cellars. Some did an experiment. They took out the mud from an old cellar and mixed it with that of a new cellar, resulting in an enhancement in maturity of the new cellar, and in an improvement of the quality of the wine fermented there.

This experiment indicates that the microbe family plays a pivotal role in the balancing of the mud. This is why Sichuan liquor enjoys worldwide fame, and out of the several top Chinese liquor brands six of them are Sichuan brands.

Among the dozen famous Chinese liquor brands Sichuan liquor brands account for half of them. Why? I think this can largely be attributed to the mud cellars of us Sichuanese.

To people's amazement, ancient pot

The Restored Ceramic Jars

ale was discovered in the ancient wine cellar unearthed at Shuijing Workshop. Scientists separated the special microbes from the brewing environment of Shuijing Workshop with the help of modern microbiological technology, and activated and reproduced the ancient pot ale microbe group. This group is named "Microbe No. 1 of Shuijing Workshop". Presently, scientists in Chengdu are still carrying out this interesting research. Perhaps some day in the future we will be able to taste the wine brewed in our ancestors' hands.

The people in Chengdu have inherited the lifestyle of theater-going and tea-drinking. No matter how greatly the city may have changed, Chengdu has always retained a unique leisureliness and joviality.

The nature of the Chengdu people may stem from the advanced geographical conditions. The expanse of Chengdu Plain enjoys a moderate climate and abundant rainfall. It is famous as the "heavenly state" for its freedom from the vigor of winter and from the intense heat of the summer.

The abundant resources have given rise to the booming development of the brewing industry. The history of Sichuan liquor is almost as long as that of the Central Plain. At the Baodun cultural site of Sichuan many utensils related to liquor were excavated, and at the famous sites of Sanxingdui and Jinsha, many wine vessels were also unearthed.

The Ceramic Fragments

The discovery of the brewing site of Shuijing Workshop has further enriched the history of Sichuan liquor culture. When did it start and what vicissitudes has it unfolded?

It can be confirmed from the large number of ceramic fragments of the Ming Dynasty that the history of Shuijing Workshop is no later than the middle period of the Ming Dynasty. Some of the fragments have even an earlier date, possibly in the Yuan and Song Dynasties.

Chen Jian

Associate research fellow of Archaeological Institute of Chengdu, Sichuan Province, and leader of the excavation of the site of Shuijing Workshop

Why are so many ceramic fragments that date earlier than the Ming Dynasty discovered at the site of Shuijing Street Workshop? We cannot draw the final conclusion yet, but the fact can probably provide us with more historical information that dates further back.

The East Gate of Chengdu Map

Archaeologists made a careful analysis of the historical layers of the site and discovered that the three layers were built one upon another in order. Some clues indicate that they are not clearly separated from each other, but are closely related. The site is like a continuous historical book that waits for people to read and interpret.

The third layer of the air hall of the Ming Dynasty adopted different materials in different places, which indicates that it was repaired or expanded after a long time of usage. Probably it was put to use even earlier. At the No.5 cellar there is a 3cm thick grayish glutinous layer, which is evidence of the repairing and expansion of the cellar.

So here is the question. Why did people abandon the lowest layer and build up the second one? Why did people abandon the second one and construct the top one, which is still in use?

Perhaps we have to search for the answer in the history of Chengdu.

The East Gate of Chengdu is a symbol of the cultural city. The wonderful scenery at the East Gate embodies the prosperity of Chengdu throughout many dynasties. In the ancient times when waterway transportation occupied an important position, the Fuhe River and Nanhe River formed the two major economic arteries of Chengdu. Located at the jointure of these two rivers with two important wharfs, Shuijing Street was naturally a lively gathering place of merchants.

Public houses, restaurants and teahouses crowded the street, with various bar signs swaying in the wind. As early as in the Tang Dynasty, Sichuan liquor became the favorite of poets. Many famous poets lavished their praises on Sichuan liquor. Du Fu said, "Sichuan liquor is dense without equal". However, what Du Fu drank was probably brewing liquor such as yellow wine.

According to the history, Chengdu became an important source of rack supply in China in the Song Dynasty. The site at Shuijing Street was probably one of the important workshops at that time. At the end of the Song Dynasty and the beginning of the Yuan Dynasty, the flames of war destroyed this place. In addition, the strict liquor prohibition of the Yuan Dynasty resulted in stagnant liquor production.

Ancient Wine Workshop

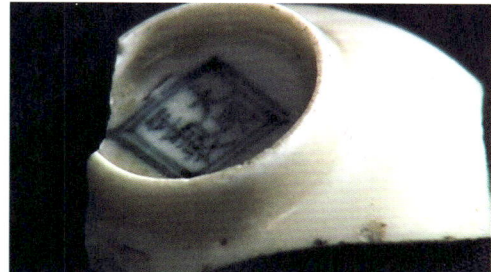

The Celadon Fragments

Towards the middle and later period of the Yuan Dynasty, with the combination of the new techniques of liquor distillation with the local ones, people began to distill liquor in a way similar to that of the modern times. As the place is far away from the central government, Shuijing Workshop of Chengdu began to produce liquor in secret, and such production developed to a peak in the Ming Dynasty.

The owner of this workshop had perhaps become a local personage. The Ming relics that we can see at the Shuijing Street Site are the remains of that period.

Many celadon fragments unearthed at Shuijing Workshop were from Jingdezhen in Jiangxi. The characters on the fragments indicate that they were made during the Ming Dynasty, which coincides with the peak of Jingdezhen ceramics. However, due to the geographical distance and transportation difficulties, no celadon fragments of this period had ever been unearthed in other places of Chengdu.

Duan Yu
Research fellow of the Historical Institute of Sichuan Academy of Social Sciences

Why did the owner of Shuijing Workshop take so much trouble to import such a huge batch of precious ceramic wares from Jingdezhen? It reveals two facts. First, the range of the economic and cultural exchanges in Chengdu was very wide and extended to the middle and lower reaches of the Yangtze River. Second, the owner of the workshop was indeed very wealthy. Perhaps it was he who led the trend of inter-provincial economic exchanges in Chengdu.

The Celadon Fragments with the Two Characters of "Jinchun"

Chinese Archaeological Discoveries

The Celadon Plate Restored with the Three Characters "Imperial Mark of Chen"

On one of the fragments there were the two characters of "Jinchun". According to historical records, in the Tang Dynasty, there was once a famous liquor brand called "Jinchun Rack" that served as tribute to the imperial court. The workshop of the Ming Dynasty had perhaps inherited this old brand.

On this piece were inscribed three characters, meaning "Imperial Mark of Chen".

Chen Jian
Associate research fellow of Archaeological Institute of Chengdu, Sichuan Province, and leader of the excavation of the site of Shuijing Workshop

This celadon plate has been restored. Its pattern is the typical "fisherman, axeman, farmer and scholar" one. The three characters were inscribed with diamond. We made a careful analysis of it and determined that it was produced in the middle of the Qing Dynasty during Emperor Jiaqing's reign in Jingdezhen. This is also a rare treasure that we have discovered in Chengdu.

However, this "Imperial Mark of Chen" poses great puzzles to archaeologists. In ancient times, the imperial mark is exclusively reserved for the imperial family. How could such a small liquor workshop dare to be so arrogant?

Duan Yu
Research fellow of the Historical Institute of Sichuan Academy of Social Sciences

We inferred that the workshop once produced liquor of tribute, because the imperial mark must be conferred by the court. Not everybody can give such a mark. Since this shop uses so many high-rate precious ceramics as the tableware and drinking vessels instead of the locally produced ceramics, which is not so with other cellars discovered in Chengdu, we conclude that Shuijing Workshop with the "Imperial Mark of Chen" was a first-rate restaurant at that time.

This pattern can give us some idea about the prosperity, the clamor and the unique scene of the Shuijing Workshop.

However, towards the end of the Ming Dynasty, the flames of the farmers' uprising spread through the entire Chengdu city.

The workshop of the Ming Dynasty was probably destroyed by fire and later abandoned. This is perhaps the finale of the third historical layer, the Ming relics, of the Shuijing Workshop site. Then, how did the second layer, that is the Qing relics, come into being?

According to legend, at the beginning of

Ancient Wine Workshop

the Qing Dynasty, someone from outside Chengdu came and changed once more the fate of this place.

Li Wenhua
Official of the office for the Protection of the Site of Shuijing Workshop

It is said that at the beginning of the Qing Dynasty, a Mr. Wang from an old, well-known family of liquor brewage in Shaanxi came to Chengdu. He saw the relics of Shuijing Workshop and thought it a treasure land for liquor brewage. So he bought the land and began liquor production.

To produce better wine, Mr. Wang inherited the production techniques of the old workshop and set out to search for a water source with the highest quality, since water, also known as the "blood of wine", was regarded as the key to the quality of wine.

Later, Mr. Wang found a well not far from Shuijing Shop. The water there was especially suitable for wine brewage. So he had workers carry so much water from the well that the reduction of water aroused protests from the neighboring inhabitants.

This well is said to be dug by the popular poetess Xue Tao in Chengdu. It is therefore named "Xue Tao Well".

Mr. Wang was a smart businessman. He even named the liquor "Xue Tao Liquor". The good wine, combined with the popularity of the beautiful poetess, made the workshop instantly famous. People later wrote a poem, which reads, "the charms of the beauty have indeed rendered the wine most intoxicating".

The workshop of the Wang family inherited the old brands such as "Jinchun Rack", "Imperial Mark of Chen", and developed such new brands as "Xue Tao Liquor". Mr. Wang had an increasingly booming business.

Hundreds of tableware and drinking vessels were unearthed at the Shuijing Workshop site. Among them, this small cup with the shape of a bull's eye attracts much attention. Due to the small size of the cup, it is said that some guest even swallowed it while drinking.

A very, very small cup with the weight of a dozen grams.

Lin Xiang
Professor of the Archaeological Department of Sichuan University

This cup is impossible for use at a wine workshop. It can only be used at a bar, when a banquet is held and a drinking game is played. Normally people would not use such a small

The Small Cup with the Shape of a Bull's Eye

cup. Some of the drinking vessels were made during Emperor Chenghua's reign, others during Emperor Tongzhi's reign, and so on. So the cups indicate that the place had been in the layout of "bar in front and workshop in the backyard" in the Ming and Qing Dynasties.

At the Shuijing Workshop site some stakes, bases, as well as well-preserved stone staircases and aprons were discovered. These archaeological evidences prove that there was once large construction around the workshop. It is inferred that there was the bar overlooking the street, where orthodox liquor was sold.

From the restored map, we can clearly see the grandeur of the workshop. The unique roof was for the emanation of the steam. In the spacious workshop workers plunge themselves in liquor brewing, and customers come and go at the bar in the front. The customers include individual guests who came to savor the liquor and many big customers who came to purchase liquor in a large quantity. It is said that the liquor of Shuijing Workshop was famous in Chengdu and all the major restaurants in the city attracted guests by selling liquor from Shuijing Street.

Li Wenhua
Official of the office for the Protection of the Site of Shuijing Workshop

How big was the scale? Judging from the area of the site of Shuijing Workshop and measuring according to the input capacity of the wine cellar nowadays, we infer that the annual output of Shuijing Workshop during the Ming Dynasty was as high as five to seven thousand kilograms.

Since only a small part of the site of Shuijing Street was excavated, there are probably other cellars that have not been discovered. If this is proved the case, the manufacturing capacity may be even greater.

However, such a scene of prosperity also experienced ups and downs. The archaeological discovery indicates that the air halls during the Qing Dynasty also used to be abandoned for a time. What caused its closure?

The Ancient Architecture of Chengdu Composed of Wooden Structures

Ancient Wine Workshop

The Map of the Shuijing Street

It is said that during the reigns of Emperor Qianlong and Emperor Tongzhi, Shuijing Workshop suffered from a great fire. The ancient architecture of Chengdu is mostly composed of wooden structures that cannot possibly withstand fires, whereas the dense liquor in the workshop is especially liable to catch fire. Then, was the workshop of the Qing Dynasty destroyed by a fire? Though still without a clear answer, archaeologists are somewhat enlightened with a legend about the Shuijing Street.

Duan Yu
Research fellow of the Historical Institute of Sichuan Academy of Social Sciences

It is said that Shuijing Street enjoyed great prosperity at that time. There were various kinds of facilities such as bars, restaurants and so forth. Due to the prosperity and the advanced commerce, the place is very easy to catch fire. So there is a well in every courtyard.

Even with the protection of wells, people were generally helpless in the face of a sudden fire.

Li Wenhua
Official of the office for the Protection of the Site of Shuijing Workshop

The experienced workers say that around the reign of Emperor Tongzhi in the Qing Dynasty, on a cold winter night, a customer came to Shuijing Workshop to buy liquor from far away. The shop was about to close since the liquor of that day was sold out, but the owner of the workshop was touched by the sincerity of the guest and opened the storeroom to fetch liquor for him. As soon as

Chinese Archaeological Discoveries

The No.5 Wine Cellar

Two Layers of Bottoms of the No.5 Wine Cellar

the door to the storeroom opened, the fragrance of the wine blew on the guest's face. This guest was very curious and hustled to have a closer look at the many jars and pots. However, he knocked over the lantern and caused a great fire. It was windy and dry in the winter, so the Shuijing Workshop was burnt down.

This legend has perhaps revealed the reason why the Qing air halls of Shuijing Workshop were abandoned. People inferred that after the fire, the owner of the workshop reestablished it with his enormous wealth and unique manufacturing technique, and hence we have the new workshop on the top, which is still in operation today. It is exactly due to this successive operation that the underground relics were so well-preserved.

However, even the inference that the accidental wars or disasters caused the abandonment of the historical layers could not solve all the puzzles. An inexplicable phenomenon emerged at the No. 5 wine cellar.

Chen Jian
Associate research fellow of Archaeological Institute of Chengdu, Sichuan Province, and leader of the excavation of the site of Shuijing Workshop

The No.5 cellar is remarkable in that it has two doors. Here is the first door, which is located on the same plane as the air hall of the Ming Dynasty. Here is the second door, which is parallel to the air hall of the Qing Dynasty. We anatomized its interior and discovered that the cellar had two layers of bottoms. The difference in heights between the two layers coincides with the elevated height between the two cellar doors.

Why should every new layer be built higher than the previous one? Is there a particular reason for that? Some experts were enlightened with this phenomenon and put forward new hypotheses regarding the ups and downs of the Shuijing Street Workshop.

Duan Yu
Research fellow of the Historical Institute of Sichuan Academy of Social Sciences

According to the analysis, it is related to the rising of the ground water of Chengdu. Chengdu lies in an alluvial plain, which used to be an inland lake long ago and was transformed into its present shape by the accumulated bedload of Tuojiang River on the upper reach of Minjiang River due to the movement of the mountains. It therefore has a high level of ground water. Especially during summers and autumns, when the mountain torrents burst out, the ground water rose further, which had great impact upon the cellars. If the level of ground water was higher than the cellar door, the liquor in the cellars might be destroyed. So the workers had to block the cellars up. After several years, perhaps the water became higher still, and people had to block the cellars further up. Hence we have the different layers now.

Due to the limited scope of the current archaeological work, no excavations had been carried out further beneath the third layer. It is therefore highly possible that earlier cultural relics were hidden further below. There might be other possible reasons of the abandonment and reconstruction of the different historical layers, and future excavations might provide us with more reasonable answers.

In any case, the site of Shuijing Street Workshop has been the earliest workshop of Chinese distilled liquor. It was listed among the top 10 new archaeological discoveries in 1999 in China and declared

The Site of Shuijing Street Workshop

to be one of the national key units of the protection of cultural relics by the State Council in 2001. It also was awarded with a credential as the oldest brewing workshop from the Guinness Book of World Records.

The dream-like realities of ancient history have long been bygone. Chinese often compare the bygones to mellow wine. Perhaps No. 19 Shuijing Workshop brewed not only wine but also the history of over 600 years and the dense and fragrant traditional culture of ancient China.

Underground Guard of Honor

In the northwestern regions of China, there is a city called Wuwei. In the city stands an earth hummock of over eight meters high, and the local people call it Lei Tai.

On the top of Lei Tai is a Taoist temple called Lei Zu Temple. It is said that Lei Tai was a place for offering sacrifice to the Thunder God.

This story has lasted several hundred years. A discovery in the 20th century shows people a surprising world under the temple.

Underground Guard of Honor

Wuwei is an old city over two thousand years old. It is located in the middle of Gansu Province, and is over two thousand kilometers away from the capital city of Beijing.

This city, just like other Chinese cities, presents more and more aspects of a modern city. However, its past contains a distant legend of an ancient civilization.

In 121 BC, the fifth emperor of the Western Han Dynasty, Han Wu Di, dispatched his renowned military officer General Huo Qubing to go on a punitive expedition to the desolate and vast northwestern regions. After hard and fierce battles, the troops of Western Han drove away the Hun people. To show the prestige of his troops, Huo Qubing named one place his troops occupied "Wuwei".

Later, Wuwei was renamed Liangzhou, which literally means a land where it is cool. Many ancient poets wrote poems about Liangzhou. The most famous one is "A Song of Liangzhou", which says, "White clouds hovering above the Yellow River afar in the sky, a lonely city kept silent surrounded by mountains high. Qiang-flute needn't sing the tune of Weeping Willow, for the Frontier Pass shut though vernal breezes blow."

On the north of Wuwei is a vast desert, and on the south are high mountains. In the desolate landscape, Wuwei is more or less a rich and populous place. It is recorded that Wuwei was a populous place that produced abundant products.

For over two thousand years, Wuwei has always been one of the most important cities in the northwestern regions of China, and historical sites, cultural relics and graves of different times are scattered in this land of about 30,000 square kilometers.

Underground Guard of Honor

Lei Tai

Wuwei has seen numerous past events. Baita Temple, which has been partially recovered, was an important temple of Sakya of Tibetan Buddhism. In 1247 AD, the Sakya leader Saban held the famous "Liangzhou Meeting" with Kuoduan, Xiliang Governor of Mongolia. This symbolized the entry of Tibet into Chinese territory.

Compared with a range of historical relics, Lei Tai, which is one kilometer to the north of Wuwei, was not conspicuous at first. It is rectangular: 8.6m high, 106m long from south to north, and 60m long from east to west. According to historical data, Lei Tai was founded in the fourth century. At that time, Wuwei was part of a kingdom called Qianliang. In order to boost his prestige, King Zhang Mao ordered his people to build a hummock, on which grand architectures were built. However, the folklore tells a different story: Lei Tai was a place where ancient people offered sacrifices to the Thunder God. Which is true? People never tried to find out the answer. Today, the king's pavilions, terraces, and towers on Lei Tai have all disappeared, but Lei Zu Temple still stands for people to offer sacrifices to the Thunder God.

In the early fall of 1969, a casual action added a new riddle to the mystery of Lei Tai.

On September 22nd of that year, the farmers of Xinxian Village of Wuwei came to Lei Tai. They had worked for more than one month to excavate an air-raid shelter in Lei Tai. Villager Cai Yao was one of the farmers. He recollected that when he excavated to the depth of over 9m, his hoe made contact with some hard object.

Cai Yao

Villager
  My hoe hit some bricks. I removed the bricks, and found horses inside. I enlarged the hole, and got down into it.

In the faint light of flashlight and kerosene lamp, people were surprised to see very strange carts, horses and dummies placed on the brick floor. All these things were covered with green rust, and were heavy to lift. The farmers gabbled that they must be made of bronze.

Without any archaeological knowledge, the villagers put the bronze carts, horses and dummies into sacks, and placed the sacks in the warehouse of their village.

Dang Shoushan, who worked for Wuwei Cultural Center at that time, became an important figure in this event. In October 1969, he accidentally heard about the discovery under Lei Tai. He rushed to Xinxian Village, and with the assistance of the villagers, he entered into the underground world. With his rich experience, he believed that it was an ancient grave.

Dang Shoushan

Former director of Wuwei Museum
  I got into the hole to find coins everywhere on the floor. There were also potteries including pottery architectural models. As an antiquarian, I never saw such a large grave or so many coins.

From what the villagers talked about, Dang Shoushan felt there must be more cultural relics. As he requested over and over again, the villagers brought him to their warehouse.

Dang Shoushan:
  Entering into the warehouse, I saw piles of bronze carts and horses and other bronze ware. I had been engaged in the work of cultural relics for many years, but I had never seen so many important relics. I was so happy, but it was painful seeing them piled up like garbage.

Dang Shoushan sorted and counted and registered the relics at once. Then, he moved the cultural relics into the local Confucian Temple for temporary storage. In the second year, the cultural relics were officially collected by Gansu Provincial Museum.

Nobody knew what surprise this discovery would give to people.

From the Lei Tai grave, people unearthed 231 pieces of cultural relics, including gold, silver and jade ware, pottery ware, and bronze ware. On a fine bronze table, there was a cup for holding food or wine. Beside the cup were not chopsticks but forks. This was really a surprise.

Handy and practical potteries were mostly household goods. On their surface was colorful glaze. Though simple and unsophisticated, these potteries presented the atmosphere of life.

The Cooking Utensils

The kitchen range had been used in the northern countryside of China for several thousand years.

The most exciting relics were the 99 pieces of bronze ware, including 38 horses, 1 ox, 14 carts, 17 knights, and 29 slaves handling the ribbons. They looked like a team. However, their marshaling sequence had been broken, and people had to arrange the team according to historical data and memory.

In the front of the team was a distinctive horse, which was 34.5cm high and 45cm long. People were surprised by its beauty, but didn't realize its value at first.

Behind the leading horse were 17 horses and knights in three columns. The knights were majestic-looking, and held halberds in their hands.

The Kitchen Range

Behind the cavalry were carts. In the

Chinese Archaeological Discoveries

Bronze Horses and Carts Arranged according to Historical Data and Memory

The Axe Cart

The Luxury Yao Carts

front was a leading cart with a large axe, so this cart was called the Axe Cart. Behind the Axe Cart were four luxury Yao Carts, each of which was pulled by one horse. In each cart there were one cart driver and two servant girls, and in front of the carts were eight persons. Four of them were military officers and the remaining four were officials. On their backs were the inscription "servants of Zhang's".

There were inscriptions on the necks of the horses too, marking the status of their masters. The inscriptions didn't give their names, but the masters were all Zhang's family members who took various official positions.

Behind the carts were five horses. The horse in the middle was tall and good-looking. It should be the master's. The remaining four horses followed closely, and they should belong to the personal bodyguards.

An oxcart followed the whole team. It was for transportation.

The Carts with the Tail Doors

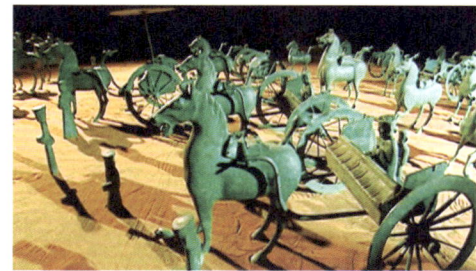
Bronze Horses and Carts

The bronze horses were very lifelike, while the carts looked just like they were real ones. You could even open their tail doors.

Apparently, it was not a fighting team, but a guard of honor. We could see that the owner of the grave was a person with honorable status. Who was he?

Today, a park has been established around Lei Tai. In the park, there are modern facilities, as well as western-style fountains and lawns. But the most attractive spot is the duplicate of the team of horses and carts, which is larger by a scale of 6. It reminds people of the past that happened here.

There is still a wonderful world under Lei Tai not far from this spot.

Tourist guide:

This grave is where the logo of Chinese Tourism, the Galloping Horse Stepping on a Flying Swallow, was unearthed. The grave is composed of a passage, a corridor, front chamber, middle chamber and rear chamber.

The long passage, corridor and chambers form a deep porch. The door of the grave is quite narrow, and people have to crouch to enter it. To prevent the grave from collapsing, the chambers have been reinforced with reinforced concrete and steel structures. Although the grave was opened over thirty years ago, there seem to be more secrets inside.

It is a large brick grave that goes from east to west, and the whole passage is 40m long.

Tourist guide:

Now we are in the grave passage. There is a very unique water well beside the passage. The mouth of the well is on the top of Lei Tai. The well is over 6m deep. What is peculiar is that whatever you throw into the well will look bigger than it actually is.

Tourist:

Actually, it does seem larger.

It has become the most popular game for tourists to throw something into the well to see it double in size.

The mouth of the well is on the top of Lei Tai. That is to say, the total depth of the well is more than ten meters. Why did the ancient people make a well here beside the grave?

The Passage of the Grave

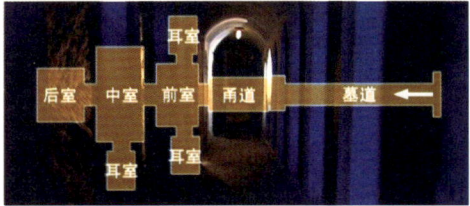

The Model of the Grave

Underground Guard of Honor

The Well of Lei Tai

Some people believe that this well has nothing to do with the grave. It was the monks who made the well for domestic water.

Dang Shoushan
Former director of Wuwei Museum
It was inconvenient for the monks to get water down the earth hummock. They made this well, so that they didn't have to go down the earth hummock to get water.

What is inexplicable is that the well wall goes down vertically all along the grave passage. Is it just a coincidence? Another argument is that the well is not only for providing domestic water, but also for positioning the grave passage, so as to position the whole grave.

But, why did the ancient people focus so much energy on the positioning of the grave?

Answers to all the questions could not be found, and neither could the chambers be accurately recovered. Above the grave door remain some traces of bricks. There should have been a beautiful door here before, from where the owner of the grave was expected to rise to heaven.

Passing through the door, we enter into the corridor and front chamber. There are two wing chambers attached to the front chamber.

It was recollected that part of the team of horses and carts was placed in the south wing chamber where the villagers entered at first.

When the chamber was just opened, there were red patterns on the walls. The color has weathered and disappeared. Today, we can only see some vague patterns of lotus on the ceilings of the middle chamber and rear chamber. However, we can see diamond patterns composed of gray bricks on the walls of all chambers. When the grave was built, it should have been a colorful underground world.

At the west end of the grave is the rear chamber of the owner. There are four duplicates of cultural relics. They look like tortoises made of stone. Actually, they are not tortoises, but sons of dragons. Their responsibility is to carry heavy things. They once carried the coffin of the owner of the grave.

115

The Interior of the Chamber

Lotus Patterns on the Ceilings of the Chambers

Dang Shoushan
Former director of Wuwei Museum

When the rear chamber was opened, the coffin was moved to the side. What people saw included a piece of leg bone, and four stone tortoises. There was nothing else.

What had happened to the grave? Why was the body of the honorable owner lost? Was it personal enemy or greedy grave robber who had entered into the grave?

When people unearthed the grave, they found two robbers' holes, one at the door and the other in the middle chamber.

Wei Huaiheng

Researcher of Gansu Provincial Cultural Relics and Archaeological Research Institute

It was a round robber's hole with a diameter of less than one meter, to be more exact, 70-80cm. The hole was closed up with bricks.

The round hole from the robbery is in the middle chamber. It has a slant of 45 degrees and can hold just one person. The structure of the brick grave completely depends on the pressure between the bricks, and there isn't any support. Therefore, it is very difficult to dig a hole in the grave. If the angle of the hole is not suitable, the grave may collapse. However, the robber's hole was just right. That is why some people guess that the robber was probably the grave builder. Because he knew the grave like the palm of his own hand, he entered into the chamber easily.

But, why didn't the robber take away all the treasures, particularly, the precious bronze carts and horses?

Dang Shoushan:

The robber took away some gold and silver and some precious goods, and left a large

The Tortoise-shaped Stone Sculptures

amount of bronze ware. Then, he closed the hole of the robbery. This indicated that he would come back to rob the grave again.

Nobody knows what happened, but the robber didn't come back. So, the secret robber's hole and the grave were covered under the ground for thousands of years.

In the spring of 1996, 27 years after Lei Tai Grave was discovered, something happened to the quiet Lei Tai. When people repaired the sunken Lei Tai, they found another ancient grave by chance, which is just several dozens of meters to the north of the first grave.

People expected to unearth another guard of honor.

To their disappointment, they found that the grave was almost empty, and all relics had been robbed. According to the burial system of ancient China, the owner of this grave should be the ancestor of the owner of Grave No.1. Lei Tai should be a graveyard of the family. Then, what was the glorious family?

According to the inscriptions on the bronze horses and bronze persons unearthed from Grave No.1, the family name of the owner of the grave is Zhang, and before the family name are some descriptive words, the meanings of which are unknown. It might indicate the official position of the owner, and some people speculate on the status of the owner of the grave according to these words.

Wei Huaiheng
Researcher of Gansu Provincial Cultural Relics and Archaeological Research Institute

My opinion is that the owner of the grave was a head of a county, because the inscriptions on the horses say so. The inscriptions on the eight horses all said "Head of Zhangye", which should be the rank. At least the inscriptions mention "one thousand people on his left side", which means he took charge of one thousand people.

A courtyard model was unearthed from Grave No.1. It is just a little bit, more than one meter high, and is composed of 23 removable component parts. There are fences around the courtyard to protect the pavilion in the middle. Did such a strictly protected courtyard belong to a head of a county?

Among the unearthed cultural relics, there are three silver stamps. On the three stamps there are three Chinese characters "Zhang Jiang Jun", meaning General.

Zhang. Therefore, some people say that the owner of the grave was not a head of a county but a general called Zhang who defended Wuwei.

Before we could determine whether he was a head of a county or a general, we should determine the time when the grave was built first. According to the tens of thousands of coins unearthed from the grave, the grave was built in the last years of the Eastern Han Dynasty.

A Courtyard Model Made of Pottery

In the last years of the Eastern Han Dynasty, Chinese society was actually controlled by the aristocrats. Several bold and unreserved families possessed absolute political power, and took the important official positions from generation to generation. According to historical records, Zhang's family was one of the most powerful families in Wuwei Area at that time. This corroborates with the inscriptions of the unearthed relics. However, there appeared new opinions about the time when the grave was built.

The Stamp With Three Chinese Characters "Zhang Jiang Jun"

Dang Shoushan
Former director of Wuwei Museum

Not long ago, some people put forward that the grave was built in Wei or Jin Dynasty, because the Chinese characters "五朱" on the unearthed coins don't have the character component "金", and only Wei or Jin Dynasty had this kind of coins. Some other people also concluded the grave was built in Wei or Jin Dynasty by analyzing the structure of the grave and the relics unearthed from the grave.

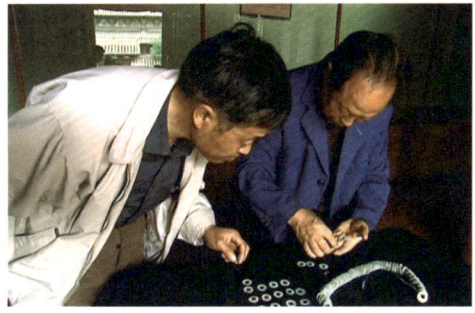
The Specialists Studying the "Wu Zhu" Coins

Wei or Jin Dynasty was not far from the last years of the Eastern Han Dynasty. In 220 AD, a local warlord dethroned the last emperor of the Eastern Han Dynasty. He came to the throne himself and founded the Wei Dynasty. Forty-five years later, the Wei Dynasty was replaced by the Jin Dynasty. However, the decline of the central dynasty resulted in the expansion of the local forces. Subsequently, the Zhang family in the Wuwei Area established the local kingdom on their own, which was Qianliang. Its capital city was right in Wuwei. According to historical records, Lei Tai was built by the first king of Qianliang.

Then, what is the relation between the owner of Lei Tai Grave and the Qianliang Kingdom? Is it possible that he was the ancestor of Qianliang kings?

Several decades have passed, and the identity of the grave's owner is still unknown. What we do know is that he belonged to the Zhang Family, and was probably a general defending Wuwei.

It is natural for a powerful general in the local area to go out with a guard of honor.

National Expressway No.312 starts from Shanghai and ends at Yili of Xinjiang. When it passes Wuwei of Gansu Province, it falls across distant history. The modern expressway and the ancient military facility, the Ming Great Wall, form an interesting junction in Wuwei. Actually,

The Junction of the Modern Expressway and the Ancient Military Facility

just several dozens of meters away from the Ming Great Wall, the relic site of the Han Great Wall extended in parallel.

Gansu was a frontier juncture where Hua Xia Nation fought against the northern nomads. The Qin Great Wall passed through here, and Emperor Wu of the Han Dynasty built a firmer Han Fort here. Even so, brutal battles frequently burst out here, and ancient poets would feel melancholy when they arrived here. One poet once sang "The cups of jade alight with wine of grapes at night. Toasting to PiPa songs, we are summoned to fight. Laugh not if we lay drunken on the battle ground. How many warriors ever come back safe and sound?"

Years have passed by. Today's Gansu is peaceful, but the historical traces are extremely vivid. History and reality cannot be separated from each other here. To the farmers here in Wuwei, discoveries such

The Relic Site of the Ancient Great Wall

as Lei Tai Grave are not rare. After being unearthed in 1969, Lei Tai Grave hadn't drawn very much attention until two years later.

In September 1971, Guo Moruo, the famous paleographer and historian, accompanied foreign guests to visit Lanzhou. When visiting the museum, he was attracted by a piece of cultural relic.

It is a galloping horse that steps on a flying swallow, and the swallow turns its head in surprise. A dreamlike moment is immortalized.

Guo Moruo, who had seen numerous precious cultural relics, was surprised at the perfect shape, lively pose and ideal balance of the sculpture.

Wei Huaiheng
Researcher of Gansu Provincial Cultural Relics and Archaeological Research Institute

Mr. Guo said, the bronze wares including the galloping horse stepping on a flying swallow unearthed from Lei Tai Grave were very important, and he would tell the National Cultural Relics Bureau about these cultural relics. Beijing was holding an exhibition of unearthed cultural relics, and he wanted to add the cultural relics unearthed from Lei Tai Grave into the exhibition.

In 1973, the galloping horse was exhibited in the U.K. and France, and drew a lot of attention. Since then, the galloping horse stepping on a flying swallow has

Underground Guard of Honor

Guo Moruo (Middle) Appreciating the Bronze Galloping Horse

The Galloping Horse Stepping on a Flying Swallow

entered into people's view, and aroused interest among a lot of people.

The research of the galloping horse at once became a hot topic, and people wanted to know what kind of horse it was. Some said it was a legendary holy horse, and was imagined and created by the artist and that it never existed in the real world.

In the artistic world, the horse is an everlasting theme of sculpture and paintings. Xu Beihong, one of the most outstanding painters in modern China, was famous for his Galloping Horses. His horses are energetic and animated, but these horses don't come completely from the imagination. To recreate the real spirit of horses, Xu Beihong went to Northwest China for sketching from nature.

The northwestern regions of China have been the home to finely-bred horses. The last group of wild horses in the world disappeared in the area where Xinjiang of China and Inner Mongolia meet.

If this horse came from the real world, what variety did it belong to? Who bred it?

The horse is one of the wild animals that man first domesticated. Long, long ago, the horse became the major tool for people to ride instead of walk. To many ancient ethnic groups, the horse was an intelligent animal.

In ancient China, horses were buried alive with the dead as glorious fortune. Many graves of aristocrats had special horse pits, where hundreds of warhorses were buried. In the cold steel period, horses were one of the most important fighting tools, and the performance of warhorses was an important assurance of the fighting capability of a troop.

Emperor Shihuang of Qin Dynasty, the first emperor of China, loved horses very much. It was said that his success resulted from the fact that his people were good at breeding warhorses. Maybe he was reluctant to kill many horses, so he substituted pottery horses for the real horses and buried the pottery horses with him. These pottery horses were of the same size as real horses.

The Galloping Horse Painted by Xu Beihong

Zhou Benxiong

Researcher of CASS Archaeological Research Institute

The pottery horses made in Qin Dynasty were characterized by thick and short legs, short torsos, and short necks. This kind of horse was hardworking and able to endure hardships, but couldn't gallop fast.

Cui Taibao

Professor of Zoic Science and Technology College of Gansu Agricultural University

These horses were used in both driving carts and riding, particularly in driving carts.

Zhaoling Six Horses, a fine work of Chinese ancient stone relievos, showed six horses in war. They were beloved horses of Li Shimin, emperor of Tang Dynasty.

The horses of Zhaoling Six Horses look quite similar to the Galloping Horse Stepping on a Flying Swallow. They are all featured by proportional torsos and long legs, which are quite different from those of the pottery horses of Emperor Shihuang of Qin Dynasty. From the pottery horses of Emperor Shihuang of Qin Dynasty to the Galloping Horse Stepping on a Flying Swallow, more than four hundred years had passed, and the varieties of horses had changed a lot. How did the changes take place?

The Pottery Horses of Emperor Shihuang of Qin Dynasty

Underground Guard of Honor

One of Zhaoling Six Horses

The horse-breeding technology of Chinese people reached new height in the Western Han Dynasty, and new varieties appeared. This owed to one of the most famous emperors in Chinese history, Emperor Wu of the Han Dynasty.

Ambitious Emperor Wu of the Han Dynasty had a personal interest, namely, breeding horses. His minister who came back from the Western Regions told Emperor Wu that there was a kind of blue-blooded horse in Dawan State, which was far away from the Han Dynasty. The emperor, who loved horses, immediately dispatched an envoy to go to Dawan State. The envoy took a gold horse of a real horse's size with him to trade for a real horse. However, the Dawan people killed the envoy and robbed the gold horse.

Emperor Wu of the Han Dynasty was furious and decided to take revenge against Dawan State. In 104 BC and 101 BC, Han Dynasty unleashed war against Dawan State twice. Before the powerful Han troops, Dawan State, to make peace, offered Han troops dozens of studhorses and several thousands of stallions and mares. Emperor Wu of the Han Dynasty became excited about these Dawan horses. To the emperor, Dawan horses were like the legendary holy horses. He proclaimed Dawan horses as "heavenly horses".

Was the Galloping Horse Stepping on a Flying Swallow a heavenly horse of Emperor Wu of the Han Dynasty, or a Dawan horse? Animal experts received some clues from the pose of the galloping horse. Three legs of the galloping horse rise high into the air, and what's more

The Bronze Galloping Horse with "Offside Pace"

surprising is that two legs on one side rise in the same direction. This is impossible for a common galloping horse.

There is a term for this pose, namely, "offside pace".

123

Cui Taibao
Professor of Zoic Science and Technology College of Gansu Agricultural University

When you ride such a horse, you don't jolt up and down, but sway from one side to another. This is quite comfortable. When the officers and soldiers rode "offside pace" horses, they could sleep on the horses. That's why these horses were very popular at that time.

Chinese Horses in Wuwei

The Galloping Horse Stepping on a Flying Swallow shows not only the characteristics of speed and stability as a blue-blood horse, but also some characteristics of Mongolian horses. It looks muscular and strong, which means it is not a pure-breed Dawan horse. In fact, when Emperor Wu of the Han Dynasty received Dawan horses, he hybridized Dawan horses with Mongolian horses, to get the unique Chinese horses.

Cui Taibao:

Horses are used in both agricultural production and wars. Chinese horses were cultivated for these two purposes. They represented the highest achievement of horse breeding in ancient China, and they combined the characteristics of two totally different horses.

In ancient times, Wuwei was a horse-breeding base, and Liangzhou horses were outstanding representatives of Chinese horses. Some experts believed that the Galloping Horse was a typical Liangzhou horse, which was strong, vigorous, and powerful. It displayed all the strong points of horses. Like a horse model, the galloping horse is the most perfect horse to Chinese people.

The disputes about the horse haven't ended, and the flying bird becomes a question. Guo Moruo believed it was a swallow, so he named this sculpture "Galloping Horse Stepping on a Flying Swallow". However, attentive people have different ideas. The tail of the bird is almost square, so the bird looks like a crow, not a swallow. Some others believe the bird is a king of birds—the eagle.

Mr. Zhou Benxiong is more attentive. He put forward a supposition: was there any bird with eyes that looked like those of an eagle, body that looked like that of a swallow, and tail that looked like that of a crow?

Zhou Benxiong
Researcher of CASS Archaeological Research Institute

Then what is the flying bird? First of all, its beak is crooked like an eagle; its eyes are big; and its tail isn't deeply forked. So it is not a

The Flying Swallow

swallow. It has long wings, and looks much like a hawk in the western regions. Therefore, I believe that the bird that the galloping horse stepped on is a hawk. Today people still domesticate hawks and use them in hunting.

The hawk, which looks like both a swallow and an eagle, flies very quickly. Particularly with its beak down, a hawk can fly at a speed of 289km/h.

Today in the western regions, people still use hawks to hunt foxes and some other small animals. Horses and hawks are both assistants to people. When they hunt, one gallops and the other flies. So, it is natural to put them together.

Although the disputes continue, the sculpture is called "Galloping Horse Stepping on a Flying Swallow" more and more frequently by people. Anyway, its beauty doesn't rest with the horse and the bird themselves, but the bold imagination and magical sculpting method. It is truly a remarkable, world-class artwork.

In 1984 the National Tourism Administration chose the Galloping Horse Stepping on a Flying Swallow as a candidate of its logo. Other candidates included the Great Wall and Giant Panda.

Tong Hualing

Managing deputy director of Chinese Tourism Association

When we chose the Galloping Horse Stepping on a Flying Swallow, we thought that this sculpture was more meaningful than the Great Wall and Giant Panda. First, the galloping horse could represent the galloping tourist industry of China, and second, it was a cultural relic that contained the long history and culture of China. So, we eventually chose the Galloping Horse Stepping on a Flying Swallow as our logo.

Today, tourists who come to China have all become familiar with the image of the galloping horse. It is not only a logo of Chinese tourism, but also a representative of numerous cultural relics of China. It has become a symbol of ancient Chinese civilization.

The Remote Kingdom of Western Xia

In the suburbs of Yinchuan, a northwestern city in China, there, amazingly, stand hundreds of round and square yellow hillocks on the deserted plain at the foot of Helanshan Mountain. Among them there are some hillocks somewhat similar to the pyramids of ancient Egypt, and hence people call them "Oriental Pyramids."

Are they mausoleums, or altars where people pray to the sky for providence? Or ancient chateaus with hidden treasures? Who built them?

The Remote Kingdom of Western Xia

Yinchuan is the capital of Ningxia Autonomous Region of the Hui Nationality. In Chinese, Yinchuan means "silver plain."

According to history, during the period between the 11th century AD and 13th century AD, there was a kingdom named Western Xia with its capital at Yinchuan in northwestern China. In that time, there used to stand splendid palaces and bustling bazaars.

On the busiest street in today's Yinchuan City, there stands a gate tower of antique style. The local people call it the South Gate Tower. The square before the tower is a place of congregation for the people. It is said that the tower existed in as early as the Western Xia period, and that the retained tower was reconstructed in the 20th century, after being tested from time to time. More than 1000 years ago, here perhaps was the central area of the capital city of the Western Xia Kingdom.

According to the local legends, these hillocks are mausoleums of Li Yuanhao, King of the Western Xia Dynasty. Yuanhao was cruel and suspicious in his lifetime. He killed people like flies. Out of the fear that his enemies should dig up his resting place, he arranged innumerous similar mausoleums to puzzle them.

Whether the legends are true or not, the mysterious hillocks were forgotten for a long time. They were exposed on the plain until archaeologists came for investigation

Zhong Kan

Former curator of Ningxia Museum
In 1971, this place was lifeless and deserted except for occasional flocks. There was no sign of modernity, only deserts after deserts.

The Remote Kingdom of Western Xia

in 1971.

At the site, people discovered many fragments with inscriptions. Some of them were Chinese characters, whereas some others were similar to Chinese characters but unintelligible to anyone. Experienced archaeologists distinguished them as ancient characters of the Western Xia Kingdom.

Judging from the remaining characters, we can be sure that this is indeed the site of the Western Xia Kingdom. Later, people found out in the historical literature of the Ming Dynasty that under Helanshan Mountain were buried several kings of the Western Xia Dynasty.

Therefore, archaeologists tentatively determined that the site here was the imperial mausoleum of the Western Xia Kingdom.

However, there were only sporadic records in the ancient literature concerning the history of the Western Xia Dynasty. No accurate or detailed records were left. What are the past and the legends of this ancient kingdom named Western Xia?

In 1908, a mysterious band of camels came to a desert in the depths of Inner Mongolia. Here were scattered some ancient relics. The local people called the place Black Water City. It was said that many rare treasures were buried here. The head of the team was a retired Russian officer named Curtzrov. He dug out a dozen cases of ancient relics and sent them all to

The Imperial Mausoleums of the Western Xia Kingdom

Russia.

In the next year, Curtzrov came again to Black Water City. In a pagoda, he almost dug out an ancient museum, the treasures including innumerous Buddha figures, Buddhist scriptures, and beautiful Tang Ka. However, the robbery-like excavation caused a huge archaeological loss. Because of it, we lost many opportunities to reveal the secrets inside.

Only the over 8000 books of literature and exquisite cultural relics preserved in St. Petersburg in Russia can tell people about a once splendid civilization. However, nobody knew at the time to whom these treasures belonged.

In 1909, a Russian Sinologist discovered a Chinese-"Western-Xia" dictionary. The puzzle of Black Water City was resolved. It was formerly a city at the peak of the Western Xia Kingdom and was destroyed in warfare and earthquakes.

The ancient kingdom of the Western Xia had thus come into people's vision, but its face had been veiled with mists.

When the imperial mausoleum of the Western Xia Dynasty was discovered, people were full of hope. Perhaps the mausoleum can tell us much about this kingdom's past.

In the summer of 1972, the archaeological

The Band of Camels led by Curtzrov, a Russian Officer

work began. However, people were utterly overwhelmed about the site.

Niu Dasheng

Research fellow of Ningxia Archaeological Institute of Cultural Relics

I felt it was spacious, deserted, and mysterious. It was unspeakable. We didn't know how many things were in the mausoleum. You couldn't see the end of it in one glimpse.

Cultural Relics of the Western Xia Dynasty Preserved in St.Petersburg in Russia

The Remote Kingdom of Western Xia

Cultural Relics of the Western Xia Dynasty Preserved in St.Petersburg in Russia

After arduous investigation, it was discovered that on this land that was 4.5 km long from east to west, over 10 km long from north to south, and nearly 50 square km in total area, there were 9 large-scale imperial mausoleums and more than 200 other mausoleums of varied size. According to historical records, there were altogether 10 kings of the Western Xia Kingdom. The last king was killed by enemies and should have no mausoleum. Therefore, it was inferred that buried inside the 9 mausoleums were the 9 kings. However, where were they buried respectively?

Before making certain of the hosts of the mausoleums, archaeologists had to number the 9 mausoleums according to their locations.

The result of the investigation shows that the shapes of all the mausoleums are more or less the same. Each mausoleum is an enclosed courtyard divided into 3 parts, the front, middle, and back, with walls of tamped earth all round.

However, what is the use of the tamped hillocks? If they used to be different from what they are today, what were they like? In addition, are there any rare treasures hidden in the underground coffin chambers of the mausoleums?

After careful consideration, people decided to tentatively excavate the No.6 mausoleum apparently without holes dug by tomb-robbers. After an excavation lasting 3 years from 1972, a 24.6-meter-deep, 49-meter-long tomb passage was finally cleaned out.

The path towards the underground palace was nearer and nearer. People

131

The Tomb Passage of the No.6 Mausoleum

became excited. What heritage would the king of the Western Xia leave us?

Zhong Kan
Former curator of Ningxia Museum

When we arrived at the coffin chamber door, I was quite optimistic. At that time on both sides of the door, there was part of a mural. Painted there was a warrior with a sword on guard. At that time, I felt that perhaps there was some hope.

However, taking a further step brought deep disappointment.

Zhong Kan:

There was only a leg bone piece on the ground. Such bones as skulls, ribs, crus bones, and hip bones were all gone. Why? Perhaps the tomb robbers took out the whole body while digging, so there wasn't much left underground.

A luxurious underground palace was only left with a few burial objects, all buried in the mud or hillocks. Perhaps they were left behind by the unheeding robbers.

You can well imagine the fate of the other mausoleums. The result of the investigation was astounding. Almost all the imperial mausoleums were left with traces of excavation. What savages were these tomb raiders? Would the grand mausoleum area leave us with nothing but regrets?

The Mural on the Coffin Chamber Door

The Effigy

The Burial Object in the Underground Palace

Fortunately there was some benefit in cleaning up the relics on the ground. A few broken human figures and stone sculptures can be determined as effigies of the civil officials and officers of the Western Xia Kingdom. What are these effigies for?

In the burial system of ancient China, there normally would be a long tomb passage before the emperors' coffin chambers. On both sides of the passage, there are official sculptures that simulate the court order. There are also some animal sculptures called stone statues that guard the authority of the dead emperors.

The experts therefore judged that these sculptures were perhaps also stone statues. However, due to the small number of the excavated sculptures and the indeterminacy of their location, the order of the sculptures has remained a puzzle.

Among the large excavated relics, the most striking ones are the few grotesque stone sculptures. They were half-human, half-animal with ferocious faces. What are they for?

Bai Bin

Research fellow of the Institute of Nationality Studies of the Chinese Academy of Social Sciences

In fact it is like Hercules, like the Four Buddhist Disciples. He carries a palace, a column base. Here is the column base, that is, the base of a stone column.

There is still controversy concerning the usage of the stone base. Some think that

133

they are for carrying the monuments, on which was recorded the king's life stories and perhaps evaluations.

However, all the monuments are lost. There were only a large number of fragments scattered in the mausoleums. When archaeologists cleaned up the No.7 mausoleum, 1775 pieces of broken monuments were excavated. Li Fanwen, a scholar on the Western Xia characters, was appointed to collate the pieces. He distinguished 16 characters out of them.

Li Fanwen

Director of Ningxia Academy of Western Xia Studies

The 16 characters were distributed in 4 lines. The first line is "Da Bai Gao Guo," the second, "Hu Cheng Sheng De." "Hu Cheng" was the title of King Renxiao in the Western Xia Dynasty. The third line is "Zhi Yi Huang Di," and the fourth, "Shou Ling Zhi Wen." This "Zhi Yi" emperor is Li Renxiao, and "Shou Ling" is the name of his mausoleum according to history. After the translation of the 16 characters, we can see that this king is Emperor Li Renxiao, the fifth emperor of the Western Xia Dynasty.

It is by exceptional luck that from only 16 characters, we have found for certain a clue of the identity of the mausoleum's host. Until this day, Shou Mausoleum has been the only one among the nine mausoleums whose master can be determined.

Although the result of the excavation falls far below our expectations, the large scale of the imperial mausoleums are sufficient in testifying to the great strength and splendid past of the Western Xia. Who built this kingdom? How did it come to its peak?

The Yellow River has been called the mother river of the Chinese nation. Similar to the Nile, Hindu River, Euphrates, and Tigris, it gave birth to the earliest civilization and intelligence of human beings.

The Half-human, half-animal Stone Sculpture

16 Characters on the Fragments

The Remote Kingdom of Western Xia

Compared with the middle and lower reaches, the upper reaches of the Yellow River is much more deserted. Deserts and gravel deserts compose most of the scenery here, which is also studded with small oases and meadows.

The rich natural meadows have always been the paradise of nomadic people. Among them there is an ancient primitive tribe that is especially good at raising sheep. Sheep are their totem. The Han people call them "Qiang people."

Among the Qiang tribes, there was a tribe named Dangxiang. They originally lived on the Qinghai-Tibet Plateau on the upper reaches of the Yellow River, and expanded later from north to east. In the 7th century AD, the Dangxiang tribe pledged allegiance to the Tang Dynasty. One branch surnamed Tuoba was especially faithful. They went through fire and water for the emperor several times. The emperor therefore gave the Tuoba branch the highest honor. He granted the leaders of the Tuoba branch the surname of Li, the imperial surname of the Tang Dynasty. The branch hence became imperial kinsmen in name.

In the 10th century AD, the once-strong Tang Dynasty perished and the central plains became chaotic. More than 50 years later, the Song Dynasty united China again, but various minorities in the north took up the opportunity to expand their powers.

The Half-human, half-animal Stone Sculpture

The Exterior of the Imperial Mausoleums

Broken Monuments

Some of them established kingdoms, and others enhanced their military forces. Among them there was the Tuoba branch of the Dangxiang nationality.

In 1038 AD, Li Yuanhao, hero and leader of Tuoba Branch, came to the throne. The kingdom was named Xia and the capital was Xingqingfu, which is today's Yinchuan. Li Yuanhao was 36 that year. The history called his kingdom "Western Xia." In the peak of the Western Xia, its territory included today's Ningxia, Gansu, the western areas of Inner Mongolia, the northern areas of Shanxi, and the eastern areas of Qinghai. The kingdom covered an area of 830,000 square km.

With their contacts with the Han culture, the nomad Dangxiang people learned agriculture and pottery and entered agricultural civilization. However, traditional animal farming was still an important production method of Dangxiang people.

The discovery in the No. 177 tomb of the Imperial Mausoleum of the Western Xia Kingdom has testified to this point.

This gold-plated bronze bull is as big as a real one. It weighs 188 kg. It was founded in bronze with the surface plated with pure gold. This is one of the most exquisite objects of the Western Xia Dynasty left to posterity. The posture of the bronze bull is natural and lively. Obviously, its founder

The Stone Sculpture of Li Yuanhao

was very familiar with the posture and behavior of bulls.

Not far away from the site of the gold-plated bronze bull, people discovered a large stone horse. The horse was carved in the round with simple freehand strokes. Its style is bold and unsophisticated.

Du Yubing

Vice director of Ningxia Archaeological Institute

It is actually a representation of a life-like scene. Some say that bulls and horses are a symbol of the semi-agricultural, semi-pastoral economic form of the minorities. It happened that the bull faced inside and the horse outside. Such a placement with one statue inside and the other outside opposite to each other means, when they went out, they grazed, and when they came back, they farmed.

There were many legends about the Western Xia Kingdom, but archaeological work can give us more exact knowledge.

The Mural on the Coffin Chamber Door

For the past 30 years, the archaeological work on the Imperial Mausoleums of the Western Xia Kingdom has never been interrupted. However, the puzzles of the kingdom have not been completely solved.

In 2000, people began a protective excavation to the No. 3 mausoleum. This grand project was not finished until

A Large Stone Horse

The Gold-Plated Bronze Bull

137

2003. The excavated area was as big as over 30,000 square meters, and 140,000 construction and decoration components were excavated.

Because most of the components were broken when excavated, almost all of them needed repair. After procedures including cleaning, collating, reshaping, refilling, people had a chance to look at the artifacts of the former Dangxiang people several centuries ago.

Nowadays, from the murals of some Buddhist grottoes and the Western Xia tombs, we can still see the images of the former Dangxiang people. They look more or less the same as the people in the central plains. However, they lived on the grasslands and deserts for a long time and inherited the nomad people's nature. They were dark-skinned, bold, and stubborn. They were good at horse riding and shooting, and admire such qualities as faithfulness and pertinacity.

The Part of the Construction of the Western Xia Kingdom

The Construction Components

Despite the few varieties of the excavated cultural relics, they were enough to show the aesthetic ideas of the Dangxiang people and reveal their secrets.

The dragon has been the ancient totem of the Chinese nation and came to be loved by the surrounding minorities. Compared with the ones in the central plains, the dragons of the Dangxiang people look more ferocious and malicious. Their postures are free from restraint, which shows a unique characteristic of this nationality.

Since they lived at the communication juncture between eastern and western China, and with the ancient "Silk Road" passing through the Western Xia Kingdom, the Dangxiang people showed a keen consciousness of cultural communication. They had kept close contact with the Han and Tibetan nationalities.

Bai Bin
Research fellow of the Institute of Nationality Studies of the Chinese Academy of Social Sciences

The kingdom of Western Xia was also a multi-

The Remote Kingdom of Western Xia

ethnic country. Its culture was diverse, and the Han culture was predominant. You can well imagine the multiple ethnicities of its ministers, including the prime minister. If a prime minister could not realize his ambitions in the Song Dynasty, he could well be appointed as prime minister here.

The rich and deep central plain culture became the major spiritual resource of the Western Xia people. They established, according to that of the Song Dynasty, a political and legal system with imperial power as its center, and translated a large amount of classic Chinese literature. They even attempted to rule and unite the kingdom with Confucian ideas. With the lapse of time, Western Xia people gradually moved towards the Han civilization and finally melted into ancient Chinese culture.

The religious scene of this city perhaps represented the good hopes of human beings' harmonious existence with each other. In today's Yinchuan, disciples of Catholicism, Islamism and Buddhism can respectively find their spiritual shelter. Although the three major religions stemmed from different countries at different times and have different ideas and scriptures, here they are living together peacefully.

During the reign of the Western Xia, Buddhists dominated the city. There were all kinds of pagodas everywhere. Since their contact with Buddhism, the Western

The Images of the Western Xia People on the Tomb Murals

Xia people devoted all their passion and faith to it. They built innumerable pagodas and temples, sent for Buddhist scriptures in Tibet and the Song Dynasty, and kept digging grottos on dangerous cliffs for years.

The archaeological discoveries further proved the Western Xia people's admiration of Buddhism. Buddha is the symbol of the Western Xia culture. In St. Petersburg Museum in Russia, there is a two-headed figure of Buddha discovered in Black Water City in Inner Mongolia. It boasts of a masterpiece among the figures of Buddha all over the world. Though with two heads and four arms, the Buddha is a perfect integral body viewed from any direction.

Buddhism has melted into every aspect of the Western Xia people. In fact, many construction components excavated from the Imperial Mausoleum are related to the Buddhist faith. This animal called the sea lion has its origin in Buddhist scriptures. It is a celestial beast that can brave the ocean waves.

The Fish with Wings Being a Celestial Beast of Buddhism

The fish with wings is also a celestial beast of Buddhism. It is regarded as a spirit of water, the origin of life, and symbolizes the danger and perversity of the sea.

This is the first time that the archaeologists encountered such objects in excavation. There were altogether more than 100 pieces made of pottery and green glaze. Simply viewing the head, it is a normal Buddha figure, whereas the only difference is that the noses of many Buddha figures were arbitrarily pressed down. There were clearly even fingerprints of the workmen.

Du Yubing
Vice director of Ningxia Archaeological Institute

I think this had to do with the psychological state of the workmen at that time. For instance, Asians' faces look very smooth. Their contours were relatively flat. So perhaps according to their aesthetic ideas, they would think that a pointed nose was not beautiful.

"Jia Ling Pin Jia"

This is the recovered image of the

The Remote Kingdom of Western Xia

Buddha figures. They have mysterious and kindly faces, but starting from the stomachs, their shape becomes animal-like. Their lower limbs are stout bird legs stepping on flowing clouds.

Some compare it to the mysterious Sphinx before the pyramids. Its name is "Jia Ling Pin Jia," a celestial bird recorded in Buddhist scriptures. It is said that before coming out of its shell, the bird can talk about Buddhist scripture.

The serene and mysterious Buddhism has brought comfort to the Western Xia people's hearts. The arduous centuries-long migration, cruel warfare, diseases and death became bearable in Buddha's smile. There is still hope within endless tortures.

"Jia Ling Pin Jia"

The Wuwei area in Gansu used to be the territory of the Western Xia Kingdom. Here, quite a few relics of the ancient kingdom have been discovered. 200 years ago, right at this Dayun Temple in Wuwei, a visiting scholar discovered that there was a stele pavilion filled with bricks. The monks told him that there was an ominous monument inside. It would bring about disasters once the world saw its face. Under the repeated request of the scholar, the bricks were finally removed, and the precious secret monument came to light.

The disasters did not happen. There were only several strange characters inscribed in the monument. They looked very much like Chinese characters, but the erudite scholar could not understand a word of it. When he went around to the back of the monument and saw the Chinese characters there, the scholar resorted to the recorded title of the emperor's reign and finally came to know that the characters on the front were the long lost Western Xia characters.

This monument has now been kept intact in Wuwei Museum.

A century after the discovery of the Western Xia monument in Wuwei, the adventurer Kurtzrov discovered a large amount of Western Xia literature in Black Water City. Western Xia characters became

The Western Xia Monument at Dayun Temple in Wuwei

a burgeoning international subject and scholars from various countries have attempted to interpret their meaning. Up to now, more than 6000 Western Xia characters have been discovered.

However, the meaning and pronunciation of Western Xia characters have not been completely understood to this day. When did they originate, and how did they evolve?

It is said that at the establishment of the kingdom in 1038, Li Yuanhao proposed to design their national characters. The minister Yeli Renrong invented Western Xia characters according to the emperor's ideas.

Concerning the shape, the Western Xia characters are quite similar to the lesser seal style around the 2nd century BC. With the innumerous lines superposing each other, they are even more troublesome to write than the lesser seal style. The Western Xia people might never imagine that it is due to the complexity of their characters that they became lost later in history.

Li Fanwen
Director of Ningxia Academy of Western Xia Studies

At that time, translation was highly developed. It can be said that every temple in the area had classics in Western Xia characters. Therefore, the invention and establishment of the Western Xia characters played an important role in the politics, economy and culture of the Western Xia Kingdom.

After nearly 100 years of development after their establishment, the Western Xia characters gradually matured. A large

The Remote Kingdom of Western Xia

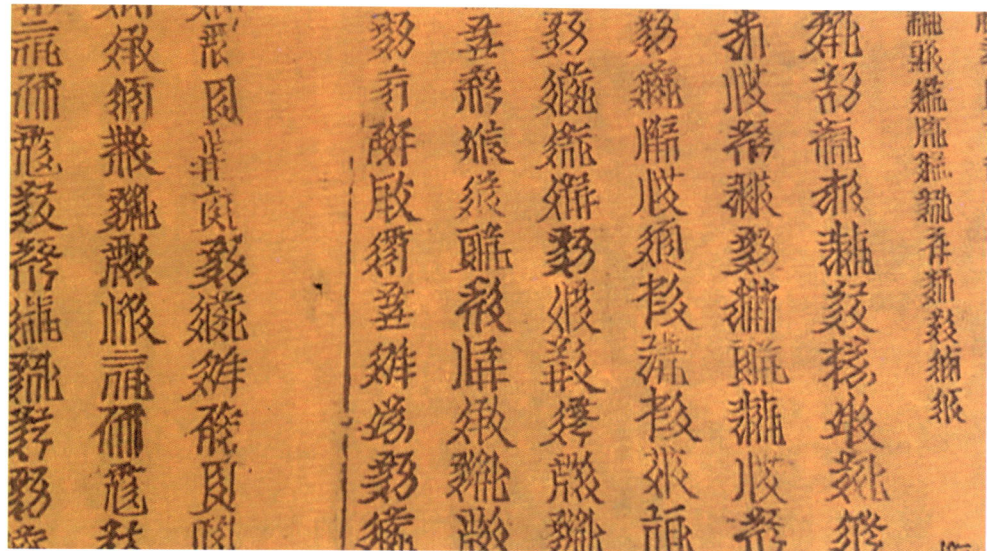

The Classics in Western Xia Characters

amount of Western Xia literature appeared. There is a complete list of literature ranging from state laws, official documents to Buddhist scriptures and literary and historical works, even to private contracts and receipts. Some of the literature was written by hand and some was printed with wooden blocks. However, there are still some other puzzling works.

Sun Shouling in Wuwei Museum loves seal carving and has a deep understanding of the characteristics of wood and clay. At the first sight of the "Analects of Wei Mo Jie" in Western Xia characters, he could tell from his experience and instinct that the record was printed with the clay types. To prove his theory, he spent 3 years in printing a new "Analects of Wei Mo Jie" with clay types.

Sun Shouling

Former vice curator of Wuwei Museum

The clay types are not straight either horizontally or vertically, because the carving was done with a rising stroke. Due to the fast turning of the knife, the characters are skewed. This is a major characteristic of clay types and can be seen at the junctures. But this will never happen to metal or wooden types.

In Yinchuan, Niu Dasheng of the Ningxia Archaeological Institute examined carefully another Buddhist scripture in Western Xia characters. He thinks that this scripture was printed with wooden types. The irregularity of the frame and the

The Duplicate of Western Xia Characters in Clay Types by Sun Shouling

The Buddhist Scripture in Western Xia Characters Printed with Wooden Types

appearance of the upside-down characters are the best proofs of the type printing.

Niu Dasheng
Research fellow of Ningxia Archaeological Institute

If this were printed with blocks, an upside-down character especially would have a special meaning. It would be intentional. But as for printing with wooden types, this upside-down character is unintentional. The difference between them is crucial.

In about the 5th century, the Chinese people invented printing with blocks, which greatly promoted the production of books. After 600 years, a craftsman called Bi Sheng invented type printing in the 11th century. However, because no works printed with types were discovered, some questioned Bi Sheng's invention.

The Western Xia literature was regarded as the earliest work printed with type printing in the world. This further proves that type printing first appeared in China and later spread to Europe through the "Silk Road."

Type printing is one of the greatest inventions in the 1000 years of human history. It provided a convenient method of media communication, accelerated the spread and accumulation of culture and knowledge, and changed, to some extent, the progress of human civilization.

Since the cleaning and repair of the No.3 Imperial Mausoleum of the Western Xia Kingdom, the once deserted place has become a hot tourist destination. The administrative office built specially two huge recovered figures of Jia Ling Pin Jia on both sides of the door. Nowadays, the spectacular figures have become a symbol of the Imperial Mausoleum of the Western Xia Dynasty.

However, to archaeologists, there are indeed few delightful surprises in the excavation and cleaning of the No. 3 Mausoleum. Through those 30 years, people have accumulated bits of knowledge about the burial of the Western Xia Kingdom in their arduous and careful work.

The most prominent building in every mausoleum is called the mausoleum tower.

Zhong Kan
Former curator of Ningxia Museum

It is solid, tampered with soil or stones. However, on its surface, it has a terrace with eaves on each floor. Besides, it is octagonal. In fact it is very similar to a tower in appearance, and that is why we call it a mausoleum tower. On each terrace, there are still some eaves with dirt piles.

The mysterious "Oriental Pyramids" have been finally recovered to their former shape. Their shape is like that of great splendid pagodas. As the highest building of the mausoleum area, the mausoleum tower is like a silent guardian that overlooks the whole area.

The mausoleum tower puzzles people. Why were such high piles of earth built in the mausoleum?

In traditional Chinese imperial mausoleums, there are usually high piles of earth on the

Cultural Relics from the Imperial Mausoleums of the Western Xia Kingdom

The Imperial Mausoleums of the Western Xia Kingdom

top of the underground coffin chambers. The earth can protect the chambers very well. Are these piles of dirt in the Imperial Mausoleums also used for this purpose?

Du Yubing
Vice director of Ningxia Archaeological Institute

We first thought that it was something like the dirt piles of the Song Mausoleums. But it turned out that wasn't the case. First the chambers are not directly under them, but in front of them. The second thing is that the buildings are not tampered purely with dirt.

Through the studies on the No.3 Mausoleum, people finally worked out the structure of the imperial mausoleums of the Western Xia Kingdom. The shape of all the imperial mausoleums is almost the same.

The outer round of the square mausoleum is the rampart. Entering the mausoleum, we can see two magpie platforms on the eastern and western sides. There is also a stele pavilion. Walking past the pavilion, we come to the moon-city with walls on three sides. Behind the moon-city, there is the mausoleum city, in front of which is the sacrificial palace. The slope-shaped tomb passage hidden underground and the kings' underground palace are located at the back of the sacrificial palace. The majestic mausoleum tower is behind the underground palace.

This form is unique in the burials of ancient China. There is yet no exact answer to why the Western Xia people designed the city in this way. The only thing for sure is that it is related to their worship for Buddhism.

People are also interested in the identity of the master of the No.3 Mausoleum. Some boldly inferred from the burial system recorded in literature that the host of the No.3 Mausoleum was Li Yuanhao, the founding hero of the Western Xia Kingdom.

It was under Li Yuanhao's leadership that the Western Xia Kingdom was established and took its hold in the northwestern areas. Li Yuanhao was a practical politician and a keen militarist. He was heroic, courageous and subtle. He is one of the greatest Dangxiang people. However, Yuanhao in his old age indulged himself in luxuries and took no care of political affairs. Even his sons hated him.

Bai Bin
Research fellow of the Institute of Nationality Studies of the Chinese Academy of Social Sciences

He has 6 to 7 wives, or 7 to 8. It was said in the drama that the final tragedy of Li Yuanhao lied in his robbing his son of the latter's wife and that his son finally killed him. So it is recorded in history. Perhaps it is true.

What cruel past had happened in this land? Was it warfare or revenge? Was it invasion by other tribes or rebellions? How could they spoil and destroy such magnificent treasures?

In the 13th century AD, there rose a valiant nomad nation, the Mongolians of the Mongolian grasslands in North China. Their leader, Genghis Khan is a legendary figure in world history. Under his leadership, the Mongolian tribes were united and formed the strongest army in inland East Asia. This army moved about, fought freely, and swept away all obstacles. They even fought with European countries at a great distance from the homeland.

Since the beginning of his conquering of the world, Genghis Khan had been attacking the Western Xia Kingdom. However, he

The Relic Site of the Imperial Mausoleums of the Western Xia Kingdom

met with unexpectedly strong resistance on this small land. In 22 years, Genghis Khan waged 6 large-scale wars against Western Xia. He himself personally commanded several military operations. But the Western Xia people resisted the attacks.

The angry Genghis Khan ordered that on the very day when he conquered the kingdom, he would kill all Western Xia people and destroy everything in the kingdom.

In 1224, the Mongolians began their attack on the bustling Black Water City. The soldiers and civilians fought for 3 months and almost all 10,000 soldiers were killed. When the city fell into enemy hands, there was not a single one who surrendered.

Genghis Khan, who conquered more than 40 countries, did not see the perdition of the Western Xia Kingdom even at his own death. In 1227, he died in the expedition towards Western Xia.

At this time, the Western Xia Kingdom was also near expiration. Not long after, the last king of the Western Xia Kingdom had to go to the station of the Mongolian general to surrender.

To fulfill the last wish of Genghis Khan, the Mongolian troops began unrestrained slaughter and destruction when they entered the capital of the Western Xia Kingdom. The fruit of this civilization was ruined in an instant, and countless innocent Western Xia people were cruelly killed.

The 190-year-long Western Xia Kingdom perished.

Traces of the Dangxiang people of the Western Xia Kingdom were gradually lost in historical change. Most of them became Han or Mongolians. The stories of their ancestors were forgotten and the past became legends.

The Western Xia characters were still used for cultural communication. Until the 15th century AD, there were still monks who inscribed scriptures in Western Xia characters. The two monuments inscribed in 1502 have become our latest discovery of the appearance of the Western Xia characters in history. Later, the 400-year-long Western Xia characters were gradually forgotten and became a "dead language."

Regardless of the dead characters or the mausoleums in ruins, the ancient kingdom of Western Xia has still been held as a special attraction for many people. Its tragic perdition and former splendor have legendary charms. People believe that this remote kingdom of Western Xia must have left many secrets for us to explore and search for.

A Palace in a Cave

In May 1968, a military engineering team in Mancheng County, Hebei province carried out a mission on a mountain. They chose the eastern slope of the main peak to cut a tunnel in. Having advanced a dozen meters, they had to use explosives again.

After a deafening blare, the engineering team walked inside the tunnel. To their amazement, they discovered that there were few stones piled up in the tunnel. Where had all the stones gone? After a careful examination, people discovered a deep cave at the site of the explosion.

A Palace in a Cave

Chinese Archaeological Discoveries

Mancheng is a county in central Hebei province, lying on a smooth plain. 1.5 km southwest to the county there is a 236-metre-high hill with the strange name of Lingshan, that is, "Tomb Hill".

Near the hill there are also two villages named Shouling, that is, "Tomb Watcher". All the seniors in the villages said their ancestors were safeguards of tombs. But for a long time no one could tell for whom they were keeping vigil or where the tomb was.

Wang Wenkui
Former Director of Administration of Cultural Relics of Mancheng County

We only know that this is Tomb Hill. Why it's Tomb Hill, no one can tell.

Cui Yaowen
Villager of Shouling (Tomb Watcher) Village of Mancheng County

I only know that it's "Tomb Watcher", but don't know whose tomb it is.

Wang Shuangyin
Villager of Shouling (Tomb Watcher) Village of Mancheng County

Even the oldest man here can't tell why the village was named "Tomb Watcher", why it's here, or whose tomb it is.

There are in fact three peaks on the Lingshan Mountain. Viewed from afar, the two flanking peaks are like the armrests of a chair, while the main peak is like the backrest, the whole shape resembling an armchair. It is said that there also used to be a limpid river at the foot of the mountain.

Such a place with mountains and rivers was regarded as a propitious place for burying the dead. Ancient Chinese

A Palace in a Cave

people thought that the tombs would have an impact on their posterity. If the ancestors were buried in a good place with picturesque scenery and abundant sunshine, the family would always enjoy prosperity.

There has always been a saying that a prince was buried in Lingshan Mountain. However, is it true? Is there an imperial tomb here? To which dynasty does it belong? No one had gone into these problems seriously for many years. The thousand-year-old puzzle was not revealed until an explosion by the local army in 1968.

The engineering team happened to discover a cave on the main peak of Lingshan Mountain and found innumerable relics in this enormous cave. The soldiers immediately reported this discovery to their superiors and the news soon passed on to the central government. The construction was stopped and an archaeological team

The Lingshan Mountain

rushed to Mancheng.

Lu Zhaoyin is a member of the former Lingshan Archaeological Team. According to him, the team directly made use of the cave discovered after the explosion and carried out excavation.

Lu Zhaoyin

Research fellow of the Archaeological Institute of Chinese Academy of Social Sciences

When we got inside, the cave was as dark as night so we couldn't see anything. We had 100-watt bulbs all round the cave but that didn't work. Later, the engineer team pulled up some electrical wire from below and we were able to straighten things out with 2000-watt bulbs, actually two 1000-watt bulbs joined together.

The archaeologists found that there were no weeds on the wall of the cave. Obviously, the cave was man-made. The experts inferred that it was an ancient tomb.

With the help of light, they saw relics of chariots and horses everywhere in the tomb. Judging from the bodies of the horses and the remains of the metal ornaments of the chariots, there were 16 horses and 4 chariots buried with the dead.

Among the chariots, there was a luxuriant "Peaceful Chariot". In ancient China, only emperors, kings and retired high-ranking officials could be privileged to have Peaceful Chariots. The presence of the Peaceful Chariot shows that the host of the tomb was a prestigious personage. Who is he? Is he a heroic general or a majestic king? Or is he the legendary prince himself?

In the northern end of the 16.5-meter-long tomb, there is a passageway from east to west. Archaeologists believed it was the path to the tomb. In the middle of the path there were two chariots. The two chariots faced the entrance of the path and seemed prepared to set out with their master at any time.

Across the path, the archaeologists entered another vault on the opposite side. It looked like a spacious storage room, with hundreds of burial objects on the ground, which made the vault more congested than the one in the south.

Lu Zhaoyin
Research fellow of the Archaeological Institute of Chinese Academy of Social Sciences

There were innumerous kinds of potteries, such as cookers, kitchenware, and kettles and urns used for storing fish. The best representatives of them were some dozen wine jars. On the jars there were characters written with cinnabar. Inside them there was wine: millet wine, rice wine, paddy wine, and superior wine.

These wine jars can contain thousands of kilograms of wine. It seems that, when alive, the owner of the tomb was a wine-lover.

Walking out of the northern room, the archaeologists walked westward along the path and entered a hall. The hall was 15 meters long from east to west and 12 meters long from north to south. The nearly-7-meter-high vault made one feel as if under open sky. On the smooth ground, there were hundreds of utensils with various usages, arranged in three sections.

The northern section was mainly composed of potteries. There were food vessels and some female tomb figures. In the southern section, there were bronze drinking vessels and lacquers such as cups and plates, as well as a lot of crossbows and iron and bronze arrows. The middle section was the most magnificent, with a row of bronze lamps with varied shapes in front

One of Liu Sheng's Chambers

of a group of stone servant-like figures. In front of the lamps there were various bronze drinking wares, kitchenware, and food vessels.

Judging from the large amount of rotten wood and rubble, there originally should have been a house with a wooden structure and tile roof in the hall, which had rotten away and collapsed. From the rotten wood, archaeologists discovered numerous bronze components with varied designs. All the components could revolve and on each of them there were inscribed numbers.

Mr. Bai Rongjin was responsible for the recovery of the relics. After careful studies on these bronze components, he confirmed that they were the components of ancient bed curtains.

Bai Rongjin

Research fellow of the Archaeological Institute of Chinese Academy of Social Sciences

It was finally confirmed that there was not only a house with four sides but also some crossbeam structures that supported the house. There were also two pieces suspended from the top, at some distance apart, forming the shape of a cross. The suspended roof looks like a ceiling. The whole set is quite exquisite.

According to the numbers on the bronze components, Bai Rongjin put them together into two brackets of big and small ancient bed curtains and recovered them.

Such luxuriant and elegant bed curtains would never belong to ordinary people. Who was the owner of them?

When putting the utensils in order, the archaeologists discovered many ancient coins. Judging from the shape of the coins, they were "Wuzhu Coins" from the Western Han Dynasty around the 2nd century BC. On some bronze wares, people also found such inscriptions as "Zhongshan Palace", "Zhongshan Inner Palace" and "Zhongshan Officials".

According to historical records, as early as in the Spring and Autumn Period

Bronze Lamps, Drinking Wares, Kitchenware, and Food Vessels

and the Period of Warring States more than 4000 years ago, there was an ancient kingdom named Zhongshan around Baoding and Mancheng in Hebei. The kingdom itself was conquered by strong enemies contending for hegemony, but the name Zhongshan still remained. In the Western Han Dynasty, the area of the ancient Zhongshan State was granted by the emperor to the feudal princes and the feudatory was still named Zhongshan.

Judging from the coins and the inscriptions on the bronze wares, the owner of the tomb should be one of the feudal princes of the Zhongshan State of the Western Han Dynasty. According to the historical records, there were altogether 10 kings of the Zhongshan State. Which one of them is the owner of the tomb on Lingshan Mountain?

From the inscriptions of some utensils, the archaeologists discovered that there were chronological records, such as 32, 34, 36, and 39 as the largest. This is to say, the reign of the owner of the tomb was at least as long as 39 years.

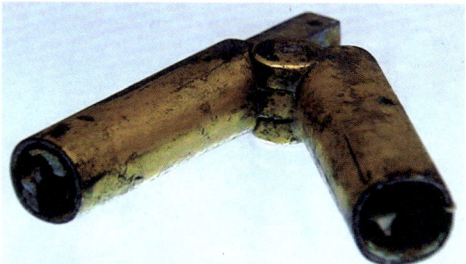

The Bronze Components of Ancient Bed Curtains

Lu Zhaoyin
Research fellow of the Archaeological Institute of Chinese Academy of Social Sciences

According to the record of *Shi Ji* and *Han Shu*, only the first king, the Zhongshan Prince Liu Sheng reigned for more than 30 years. Here we have a lot of chronological records that are over 30 years and the largest number being 39, which is in accordance with the 42-year reign of the first king recorded in *Shi Ji* and *Han Shu*.

That Zhongshan Prince was Liu Sheng, son of Emperor Jing of the Western Han Dynasty and a prestigious king. Is Liu Sheng, the Zhongshan Prince, really buried in Lingshan Mountain?

Although archaeologists had a lot of

The Recovery of the Bed Curtains

The Inscriptions on the Bronze Wares

Wuzhu Coins

clues, they were not sure yet, because the owner's inner and outer coffins had not been found.

According to the shape and structure of the tombs of ancient emperors, archaeologists predicted that there should be another back room on the western side of the middle room where the coffins were placed. However, there were only stone walls to the west of the middle room. Where was that secret back room? They groped along the stone walls. Suddenly, an archaeologist found a hidden door camouflaged in the same black as the stone walls.

The stone door indeed opened to a coffin chamber. The chamber was constructed with flagstones luxuriantly painted all over with red paint. The chamber was divided into two rooms. The side room covered about 4 square meters and stood for the bathing room, where a big bronze kettle was placed. The main room stood for the bedroom, in the middle of which there was a low desk, lamps, incense burners, as well as other articles of daily use. On the south side of the room there were various flags, weapons, and armor as if they were protecting the owner of the tomb. On the north, there was the coffin of the owner.

Lu Zhaoyin
Research fellow of the Archaeological Institute of Chinese Academy of Social Sciences

The coffin was laid on a coffin bed. The bed was made of white marble. However, after more than 2000 years, the coffin had sunk down, on top of which there were traces of thick lacquer and rotten wood.

Archaeologists carefully removed the rotten deposit in the hope of finding the remains of the owner of the tomb. To their surprise, they discovered an astounding treasure.

A Palace in a Cave

The Armor

Lu Zhaoyin
Research fellow of the Archaeological Institute of Chinese Academy of Social Sciences

  We found a complete jade suit sewn with gold thread. For more than 2000 years we hadn't known the shape of a jade suit sewn with gold thread. Neither *Shi Ji*, *Han Shu*, nor any other work record down the real shape of a jade suit sewn with gold thread. We discovered it after we cleaned everything up. It turned out to be in the same shape as that of a person, with a head, a top, trousers, two hands, gloves, and boots. The overall shape was just the same as that of a person.

  The Ancient Chinese believed that the cool, smooth, and moist jade could prevent the body from decaying. Therefore, they often put jade into or on the top of the body. In the Han Dynasty, people even made jade into suits to encoffin the dead. However, not every dead person could wear a jade suit. In the Han Dynasty, only emperors and prestigious noblemen could wear jade suits. It was also ordered that the emperors' jade burial suits be strung with gold thread, and was called "jade suit sewn with gold thread". Those of kings, prestigious personages, and princesses, were sewn with silver thread, and those of noblemen in lower ranks with bronze thread. As the system of jade burial suits was abolished at the end of the Han Dynasty, posterity had never seen a real jade burial suit other than in the records of ancient literature.

  The complete jade suit sewn with gold thread in the tomb of Lingshan Mountain was a first discovery in China as well as world archaeological history. The people on the site were very excited. However, there was also doubt: if the owner of the tomb was Liu Sheng, the Zhongshan Prince of the Western Han Dynasty, how could he,

A Jade Suit Sewn with Gold Thread in the Coffin Chamber of Liu Sheng

Chinese Archaeological Discoveries

Mr. Guo Moruo, the Famous Chinese Historian, Being in the Excavation Site

a prince, wear the jade suit sewn with gold thread that was only suitable for emperors?

The archaeologists could not determine the answer. They invited the famous Chinese historian, director of the Chinese Academy of Social Sciences at that time, Mr. Guo Moruo to the excavation site in Lingshan Mountain.

Mr. Guo carefully studied the inscriptions on the unearthed utensils and the jade suit sewn with gold thread in the coffin. According to Mr. Guo, the system of using jade burial suits in accordance with rank was not strictly carried out until the middle and late Western Han Dynasty, whereas at the time when Liu Sheng lived (in the early and middle Western Han Dynasty), the system was not carried out very strictly. Additionally, there were a lot of clear inscriptions on the articles buried with the dead, and there was no problem in identifying the owner of the tomb as Liu Sheng.

To archaeologists, it was very exciting to identify the owner of the tomb, since everything before their eyes had reached an answer. These relics covered with dust for more than 2000 years were like a time machine that brought them back to the remote past when Liu Sheng lived.

Liu Bang, the first emperor in Han Dynasty, was of humble birth. In 202 BC, he rebelled, subverted the reign of the Qin emperor, and established the Han Dynasty. However, the short-lived 16-year-long Qin Dynasty established by Emperor Qinshihuang, who unified China, also made Liu Bang's heartbeat quicken in fear.

Yue Qingping

Professor in the History Department of Peking University

He thought that only his own kinsmen who shared the same surname could be trustworthy. So, soon after the Western Han Dynasty began, he made many of his kinsmen into kings to get rid of all kings with different surnames.

At first Liu Bang conferred many rights upon the 9 kings. But with the increasing strength of the kings, they gradually posed a threat to the central power. In 156 BC,

A Palace in a Cave

40 years after the death of Liu Bang (or the Emperor Hangaozu), the "7-King Rebellion" finally broke out, in which 7 kings united to rebel against the central government.

This rebellion was quickly pacified, but emperor Jing saw the danger of development in the force of kings. He decided to take back the military force of the kings and disperse their power by dividing the feudatories into parts and conferring them to other noblemen. It was at this time that Liu Sheng was given the title of Zhongshan Prince. However, the king of Zhongshan State at this time could only enjoy the rent and taxes of the feudatory without any real power.

Yue Qingping
Professor of the History Department of Peking University

He could not exert much political power, that is to say, he was not promising in politics. So he spent much time and energy on things like the pursuit of joy.

According to the historical records, Liu Sheng was certainly a pursuer of joy. As a king, he never bothered about government affairs, but indulged in feasts, drinking wine, and seeking pleasure. He had numerous wives and concubines, as well as over 120 children.

The tomb shows clearly the extravagant life of this king. The Liu Sheng tomb in

The Bronze "Musicians"

Danghu Lamp

The Lamb Lamp

The middle room resembles the feast hall the Zhongshan King used when alive. The king sat in between the luxuriant curtains, and the guests sat on the ground, holding up exquisite drinking vessels and drinking their full and various superior wines. The maids kept passing the delicious food from the extravagant food vessels to the king and the guests. Such a feast could never do without singing and dancing. These two musicians seemed both to like singing and playing jokes, and appear to be having fun.

The feast went on as the night came. The king ordered the servants to light the lamp. Take a look at this kneeling lamb. The lamp holder is hidden beneath the back, and the empty stomach holds lamp oil. Lambs were regarded as a propitious animal in ancient times and kindling lamb lamps was a symbol of blessing. The Scarlet Bird is a legendary bird and represents the south. Kindling scarlet bird lamps symbolized auspiciousness. The name of this lamp is Danghu Lamp. Danghu is an official name for the Huns, a minority group in the north. At that time the Han Dynasty was fighting against the Hun army that invaded the northern border. The shape of a half kneeling Hun officer holding the lamp stands for the victory and prosperity of the Han Dynasty.

Lingshan Mountain is 51.7 meters long, over 37 meters wide, with the highest vault nearly 7 meters high and with a volume of about 2700 cubic meters. The arrangement of the tomb was an exact copy of a palace, with fine construction and magnificent furnishings. We can imagine his life in the imperial palace from the numerous beautiful articles buried with him.

The southern wing room, the chamber discovered after the explosion, is where the king put his chariots and horses.

The extravagant Zhongshan King had 6 chariots. From the exquisite and precious ornaments on the horses and chariots, we can imagine the splendor of the original chariots.

The four horses, armored with gilded bronze ornaments and embedded with diamonds and coral and silver ornaments, pulled the chariot, which was also made of gilded bronze ware and embedded with diamonds, gold, and silver. The colored cart had beautiful designs with various shapes. The canopy on the cart added to its majesty.

To have a ride on the elegant and graceful Peaceful Chariot is a pleasure of the king's life. Although he couldn't control the politics of the feudatory, the fragrant cart, beautiful women, and martial honor guard made him feel the honor of being a king.

One is reluctant to leave such a life of pleasure. The king did not want to lose everything after death. In order to enjoy the extravagant life eternally, he brought almost all these articles of daily use into his tomb.

This storage-like northern wing room is filled with the articles of the king's daily use. There is even a set of grindstones. At the time of unearthing, there was an animal skeleton that seemed to be the animal pulling the grindstone. It seems that the king even thought of food processing.

These bronze wares with elegant shapes were fumigators according to experts. The kindled incense can be put into the fumigators and the incense smoke rolls up through the small holes on the lids. The refreshing fragrance is thus diffused in the room.

There are many fumigators in this tomb, which shows the king's love for them.

This piece is called "Boshan Bronze Fumigator Inlaid with Gold" and is one of the most exquisite funeral objects in Liu Sheng's tomb. Boshan Mountain is, according to legends, the celestial mountain

Precious Ornaments on the Horses and Chariots

on the sea. The body of the fumigator was inlaid with gold and silver thread in fluid designs, and the finest thread is as thin as hair. It is hard to imagine how craftsmen from over 2000 years ago managed to produce such exquisite workmanship. This rare bronze ware exemplifies again the wisdom of ancient Chinese people.

This Bronze Clepsydra buried with the king is a calculagraph from over 2000 years ago. The water inside the clock trickles out steadily and the scaled wooden rule inside the clock sinks with the decrease of water. The scale can show the lapse of time. This Bronze Clepsydra is so far the earliest ancient Chinese clock besides the sundial. It is also the most ancient ancestor of modern clocks.

There is also a set of medical instruments.

This is an apparatus for measuring medicine, which indicates that the ancients had mastered strict measurements for medicine dosage. This is the medical bronze basin, which is specially used

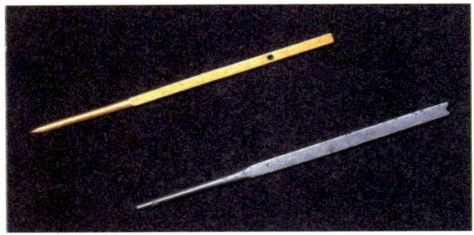
Gold and Silver Medical Needles

A Drencher

The Bronze Apparatus for Measuring Medicine

The Bronze Basin

The Bronze Clepsydra

Boshan Bronze Fumigator Inlaid with Gold

for steaming and boiling medicine or disinfection. This drencher is used for drenching the medicine into the throat or nose of the patient in emergency. There is also a bronze scalpel.

The most notable instruments are these gold and silver medical needles. Ancient Chinese invented a unique medical method, which is to cure the disease by acupuncture or moxibustion. There is a large amount of Chinese historical literature about acupuncture, but real acupuncture instruments were rarely found. These needles in Liu Sheng's tomb are so far the earliest metal needles. They are consistent with the recordings of *The Yellow Emperor's Canon of Internal Medicine* in number and shape.

2000 years ago, Liu Sheng, the Zhongshan Prince did not save his life with acupuncture. What disease did he have? Perhaps the answer can be found only through autopsy.

However, people discovered that the jade suit sewn with gold thread in the coffin was empty. Where had Liu Sheng's body gone?

Lu Zhaoyin
Research fellow of Archaeological Institute of the Chinese Academy of Social Sceinces

Mr. Guo Moruo examined it and said that the ancient ruling class often made many suspicious tombs. Perhaps this was not his real body. Perhaps his body lies beneath the jade burial suit.

The archaeologists continued digging under the coffin. But they did not find the body even in the terrain. With his rich historical knowledge, Mr. Guo Moruo predicted that there should be another tomb beside this one, and that if that tomb was not Madame Liu's, it should be where the real body of Liu Sheng lies.

After careful examination, the archaeological team discovered that there was indeed another tomb on the cliff more than 100 meters north to this one. They immediately carried out excavation. According to conventional archaeology, they started the excavation from the door of the coffin chamber. However, the door could not be opened.

The archaeologist team had to blow up the door. They discovered that the tomb passage was completely blocked with stones.

Bai Rongjin
Research fellow of the Archaeological Institute of Chinese Academy of Social Sciences

This long tomb passage was filled with blocks. Many soldiers worked around the clock and with great effort to carry all the stones out.

This tomb is more spacious. It is 41.7 meters long and 65 meters at the widest. The highest vault is nearly 8 meters. The volume of the tomb is as much as 3000 cubic meters. The arrangement is roughly the same as the previous one, and the only difference is that the back room is skewed to the southern side and does not form a straight line with the middle room.

The archaeologists discovered a bronze seal in the tomb and the inscription is "Dou Wan". According to the historical records, the wife of Liu Sheng is named Dou Wan. Undoubtedly this is the tomb of the wife of Liu Sheng.

Lu Zhaoyin
Research fellow of the Archaeological Institute of Chinese Academy of Social Sciences

The emperors and kings were, more or less, buried separately from their wives in the Western Han Dynasty. They could be buried in the same mausoleum or tomb. For example, in the Han Tombs in Mancheng County, the king and his wife were both buried in the Lingshan Mountain, but in different tombs. The chambers were separate. We call this parallel burial, the two chambers being parallel.

The Bronze Seal with the Inscription of "Dou Wan"

The Tomb Chamber of Dou Wan

The back room is skewed to the south, for Dou Wan the wife wished her resting place to be nearer to her husband.

Liu Sheng died in 113 BC, and his wife died many years after his death. Therefore, her tomb surpassed Liu Sheng's tomb in scale and degree of exquisiteness. However, due to the difference in identity, the queen's funeral objects could not be compared with those of the king.

Even in this case, the relics unearthed from Dou Wan's tomb were sufficient to give archaeologists a delightful surprise.

This is "Bronze Cup with a Sparrow Holding a Ring in Its Beak". The celestial Sparrow treads upon a monster, spreads its two wings, and holds in its mouth the glittering and translucent jade ring. The body of the bird and that of the cup were inlaid with gold thread and embedded with 30 turquoises. When unearthed, the cup still had red traces on it, which archaeologists conferred on as cosmetics. Should such an exquisite dressing case belong to a queen as beautiful as a goddess?

Perhaps she is indeed beautiful, because the lamp she used was beautiful as well.

Archaeologists called it the "Changxin Palace Lamp", because there is an inscription of "Changxin" on the body of the lamp. Changxin Palace is where the grandma of Liu Sheng, Empress Dowager Dou lived. The relation between Empress Dowager Dou and Dou Wan remains a puzzle, but it is certain that Dou Wan belonged to the family of Empress Dowager Dou. Was it because the girl was so lovely that Empress Dowager sent this rare beautiful lamp to her?

This is one of the most dazzling treasures unearthed from the Han Tombs in Lingshan Mountain. It is not only magnificent in shape but also exquisite in craftsmanship. The lamp holder in the hand of the maid-of-honor can revolve and the lamp chimney is convertible so as to freely adjust the direction and brightness of the light. The right arm and the body of the maid-in-honor are empty. When the candle burns, the ash will enter the body through the right arm without polluting the air. The ancient Chinese people knew how to

Bronze Cup with a Sparrow Holding a Ring in Its Beak

Changxin Palace Lamp

protect their living environment as early as more than 2000 years ago, which is truly amazing.

In the imperial harem filled with fair ladies, it might be rare for Dou Wan to enjoy pleasure with her husband. However, the queen had her own fun. In her tomb, people discovered a set of "Bronze Coins for Games in the Imperial Palace" and a bronze dice. This indicates that she liked playing drinking games. This bronze dice was only 2 centimeters in diameter and has as many as 18 facets. Each facet has Chinese characters inlaid with gold and silver thread and the margins are also inlaid with beautiful patterns and embedded with red agates and turquoises. This is perhaps the most expensive game apparatus in the world. We cannot imagine how the skillful craftsmen managed to inlay such complex and fine designs onto such a small area.

The bronze wine kettle is also very special. The patterns inlaid with gold and silver thread are actually artistic characters called "sealed characters". They are both the decorative patterns on the kettle and a wonderful article. The meaning is roughly as follows, "to have feasts in high spirits, to enjoy the delicious food and to let the joy flow into the skin and blood and bring about longevity." Such rich imagination and wonderful conceits are truly inspirational.

There are also many jade wares in the tomb of Dou Wan. These are jade ornaments worn on the clothes or in the hair. This Heart-like White Jade Pendant is thoroughly carved with the pattern of the fight between a bird and a beast. There is a similar one in Liu Sheng's tomb. The pattern of clouds are thoroughly carved on both sides. Putting them together, we can see that these two are a pair, which represents the mutual affinity between husband and wife.

This white and crystal-clear jade man represents the image of ancient people of over 2000 years ago. He puts both hands on the desk and seems to be working on couplets and poems or meditating. His style is cultured and genteel.

To the surprise of archaeologists, there was another jade burial suit in Dou Wan's tomb. This suit is obviously different from that in Liu Sheng's tomb in shape.

The Bronze Dice

Bai Rongjin
Research fellow of the Archaeological Institute of Chinese Academy of Social Sciences

That one was completely stitched with gold thread. This one of Dou Wan was made of larger jade pieces with no holes. They used silk bands to tie the jade into crosses and to bind the margins between the pieces. There is hemp cloth underneath to rest it on.

Heart-like White Jade Pendant

Jade Man

It is unprecedented in Chinese archaeological history to discover in one excavation two complete jade burial suits. The archaeologists were very excited. However, they were puzzled again with the ensuing discoveries.

They discovered 218 large jade pieces around Dou Wan's jade burial suit. What were they? After careful research, the experts conferred that they were probably embedded on the rotten coffin to protect the body from decaying.

According to the archaeologists' assessment, there were 2498 Xiu jade pieces and about 1000 grams of gold thread on Liu Sheng's jade burial suit, and 2160 jade pieces and about 700 grams of gold thread on Dou Wan's suit. Xiu jade is produced in Hebei with bright luster and a hard texture. The process of making a jade suit is very complex. The craftsmen had to first design jade pieces of varied sizes and shapes according to different parts of the human body, then stitch the jade pieces together with gold thread into a complete jade suit after a dozen procedures such as material selection, burnishing, perforation, polishing, and so on.

Bai Rongjin:
Take this hand for example. The glove is made to follow the lines between the fingers, the back of the hand, and the bone structure. It isn't smooth. It has angles.

It is estimated that to make such a jade suit takes a jade craftsman some dozen years and it costs the fortune of 100 middle class families.

In the tombs of Liu Sheng and his wife, there are two jade suits sewn with gold thread as well as numerous jade wares and various burial objects, which shows that the king of Zhongshan was a very wealthy man.

The Hand of Jade Burial Suit

The times when Liu Sheng and Dou Wan lived were right at the peak of the Han Dynasty. Emperor Wu expanded again and again the boundary of the country, which was even larger than the ancient Roman Empire. The Han Dynasty was very strong with an advanced civilization and many world-leading technologies.

In the tombs of Liu Sheng and Dou Wan, there were more than 600 pieces of ironware. After an examination using modern scientific methods, people discovered that the foundry standard was far beyond their original estimation. With the primitive smelting and hammering methods, craftsmen not only made cast ironware with advanced craftsmanship, but also produced "hammered steel" after hundreds of times of hammering. This is perhaps the earliest steel product in the world.

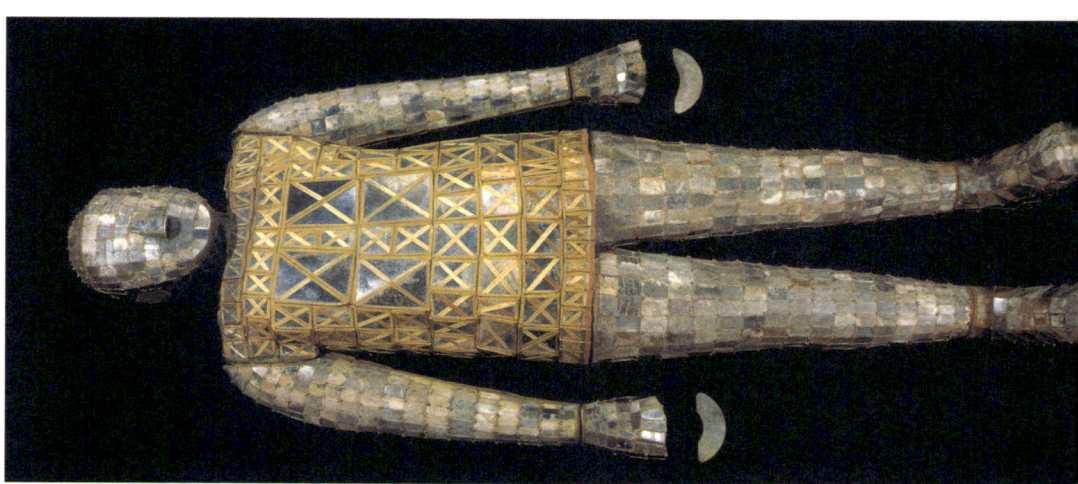

Dou Wan's Jade Burial Suit

A Palace in a Cave

Bronze Cooking Vessel with Bear Legs

The wonder of this Bronze Cooking Vessel with Bear Legs and 4 Animal-like Knobs does not only lie in its shape. The four small beasts bending over the lid are in fact part of the knob. Due to the closeness of the lid, its inner pressure becomes greater. Some people refer to it as "ancient pressure cooker".

Experts refer to these two vessels as colored glaze. Although not as hard as modern glass, it is still amazing to find the technique has had a history of more than 2000 years.

The strong dynasty brought about enormous wealth, which made the king

Colored Glazed Vessels

171

and queen of the Zhongshan State pursue immortality. They racked their brains to find a way to keep their bodies from decaying. However, the archaeologists discovered that Dou Wan's jade suit was as empty as that of Liu Sheng. Where had the bodies of the two owners gone?

In order to find the answer as soon as possible, the archaeologists started to take the gold thread apart to see what was inside.

Lu Zhaoyin
Research fellow of the Archaeological Institute of Chinese Academy of Social Sciences
We discovered human teeth. There was still a part of the Zhongshan Prince's teeth. The enamel shell of the teeth remained. There were also some broken bits of the spine, ribs, and shanks that could be vaguely recognized but couldn't be taken out. They were like mashed dates.

The expensive jade suit and the magnificent jade ware could not bring immortality to the bodies of the king and queen. In the face of death, the immortality of life was but a spiritual pursuit.

The 2-month-long excavation finally came to an end. People discovered more than ten thousand relics in the two tombs of the Zhongshan Prince and Queen Dou Wan of Zhongshan State. Although the bodies of the owners decayed, the ten thousand relics endured for more than 2000 years, from the Western Han Dynasty to today.

When people held their breath and stepped near these historical relics, almost everyone had this question in mind: how could they endure the corrosion of time?

The answer perhaps lies in the Lingshan Mountain. From days of old, emperors would generally choose a propitious place to dig deep tombs, on top of which high graves were built with a majestic imperial sleeping palace. However, Liu Sheng is different in building his grave inside a cave.

Compared with the earthen pits, the cliff tomb is well sheltered, and the temperature and humidity are suitable for preserving objects. To prevent the rainwater from leaking through the limestone, the intelligent craftsmen also built up good drainage and damp-proof systems in the tombs of Liu Sheng and his wife.

Sun Qingxiang

Senior Vice Director of the Expert Committee of China Waterproof Material Industry Association
There are several channels around it and there is a seeping well in the middle. Water is collected here and seeps downward.

This cloister surrounding the back room is also for drainage. It is connected with the

A Palace in a Cave

gutter in the middle room. Water seeping from the wall flows along the cloister into the middle room and into the seeping well through the gutter. All the tomb chambers can therefore be safe from the water.

It is not easy even with modern construction methods to construct such a huge tomb cave in the rocks. How did the craftsmen construct such a majestic cave palace 2000 years ago?

Some inferred that they first built a mountain path to transport the instruments and materials, dug a cave on the surface of the cliff on the main peak, and gradually expanded the cave from the surface. Others had different ideas regarding the limestone structure of Lingshan Mountain.

Sun Qingxiang
Senior Vice Director of the Expert Committee of China Waterproof Material Industry Association

They burnt fire under the limestone. After heating it enough, they poured water onto it. Due to the rapid change of temperature, the stone broke down into pieces.

No matter how the tombs were constructed, the Han Tombs of Mancheng County boast of a great wonder. Being built in caves allowed the tombs to elude the intrusion of thieves. Therefore, posterity is able to witness their rare treasures from 2000 years ago. It is because of this palace in a cave that the Chinese people have recovered such a long-cherished splendor.

The Mysterious Zhongshan State

In the winter of 1974, the peasants of Sanji Town in Pingshan County of Hebei Province, carried out a large-scale farmland-flattening movement. This drew the attention of the cultural relics administration, because the peasants continuously took earth from some large knolls nearby that were suspected to be ancient grave mounds. These mounds were being destroyed, so the archaeologists went to the site quickly.

Liu Laicheng, researcher with Hebei Province Cultural Relics Research Institute: When we arrived, we were surprised to see tiles everywhere on the site. The tiles were not common ones. They were big tiles used to build palaces in the Period of Warring States.

It was distressing to see the destruction of the ancient grave mounds, but it was a chance for the archaeologists to open the graves as early as possible. The Hebei Province Cultural Relics Administration approved the excavation plan promptly. Meanwhile, a peasant told Chen Yingqi, head of the archaeological team, of an odd thing.

Thirty years ago, there was an old man called Liu Ximei in the village. His farmland was being hit by heavy summer rain, so he took earth from an uncultivated place to build a bank to prevent water. When he excavated the place, he unearthed a large river stone at about half a meter deep. On the upper side of the river stone, there seemed to be characters. But nobody knew the characters, and nobody could be sure if they were characters. Several decades have passed from then.

This story aroused the archaeologists' interest. They went to Liu Ximei's home and saw the stone. Although none of them could read the characters from the Period of Warring States, they were dimly aware that they have come upon a mysterious state that disappeared over 2200 years ago.

In the 5th century BC, the Zhou Dynasty was declining day by day, and China entered into the Period of Warring States when beacon fire rose from all around and the princes would fight from time to time. During this period, an ancient ethnic group, Xianyu, continued to grow in the depths of the northern high mountains. After years of hard work, they founded their own state—the Zhongshan State. In 414 BC, the Zhongshan King called Wu Gong led his fellow citizens in crossing the Taihang Mountains. They moved to the eastern plain, and established their capital in a zone where the force of the other states was weak. However, this state was too weak. From the very beginning, it was constantly invaded by strong enemies.

Eventually in 407 BC, it was annihilated by the Wei State, one of the "Seven Powers", and became an affiliated state of Wei.

His state subjugated and family wrecked, King Huan Gong escaped into the high mountains. After reflection upon the past, he became mature. He pushed all his efforts into making his state prosperous, and accumulated force. Twenty years later, he left the mountains again and recovered his land. After that, Zhongshan State enjoyed great prosperity and powerful arms. It took part in the "Five States Jointly Acting As Prime Minister of the Emperor", and developed its territory, and the seed of envy and hatred was buried. In 296 BC, the capital city of Zhongshan State fell into enemies' hands. A state thus disappeared totally.

As for this state that experienced ups and downs, people could tell just its rough developmental history and geographical position according to fragmentary historical records, but no archaeological discoveries could prove these records. Did this "state of a thousand chariots" in the Period of Warring States disappear into thin air?

Chen Yingqi

Researcher with Hebei Province Cultural Relics Research Institute

Zhongshan State was a very small state, so there was no special record about it in history. The existing records about it were just several sentences in other history records. This was also probably because of the bias of the historians. The Zhongshan people didn't belong to the central ethnic group.

2270 years after Zhongshan State disappeared, the archaeologists saw the stone at Sanji Town, Pingshan County by accident. Was there any relation between the stone and the mysterious state? Or were the characters just an incantation? Chen Yingqi copied down the ancient characters from the stone, and sent them to Li Xueqin, an ancient character expert.

Chen Yingqi:

One week later, he replied to me. He said the stone inscription was very important, but to make doubly sure, he needed me to answer three questions first before he gave me the translation.

Li Xueqin's first question: Is there any big earth knoll in the vicinity of the stone? His second question: Is there any river or lake in the vicinity? His third question: Is there any high mountain in the vicinity?

Satisfactory answers were made to the questions. Sanji Town of Pingshan County is located in the highland at the east foot of Taihang Mountains, and to its north is the neighboring Donglin Mountain and Xilin Mountain. Also, Hutuo River passes by the town. Actually, it is a place of both mountain and river. Ancient graves gather in this place. For dozens of kilometers around, there are a large number of knolls suspected to be ancient grave mounds. Some of them are extraordinarily large. As early as in the 1950s, the local cultural relics administration numbered these hummocks. According to these characteristics, Li Xueqin affirmed the stone was a relic from the Period of Warring States, and offered the following translation of the characters on the stone.

The Ancient Characters on the Stone

"Officials Gong Cheng De and Jiu Jiang Man watch the park and the mausoleum for the king. Hereby we greet the future men of honor". These ancient characters are like a cryptograph and a piece of self-introduction Gong Cheng De and Jiu Jiang Man in the Period of Warring States left to the later generations.

Chen Yingqi
Researcher with Hebei Province Cultural Relics Research Institute

The two people wanted to tell worthy people of the future that they watched the park and fished for the king, and then protected the graves for him.

The words that these two fellows left more than two thousand years ago prove that this is a place where the ancient graves gather, and that there must have been a royal mausoleum built here in the Period of Warring States. Whose mausoleum is it then? The mysterious Zhongshan State comes to mind first.

Liu Laicheng
Researcher with Hebei Province Cultural Relics Research Institute

This place is 20 li, or 10 kilometers, from Lingshou Town. Why do I tell you this? Lingshou Town is in the territory of Zhongshan State. Therefore, the grave should be the grave of a king of Zhongshan State.

An important clue comes from this excerpt from historical records: in 380 BC, Zhongshan State moved its capital to Lingshou. How can we, with this simple record, make sure that today's Lingshou is the ancient Lingshou, capital of the Zhongshan State? If it is, can we find the relics of this ancient capital? The archaeologists carried out a large-scale field investigation of the relic site of Lingshou, the capital of Zhongshan State.

Chen Yingqi:
When Zhongshan State was subjugated by Zhao State in 296 BC, its capital was destroyed by Zhao State at the same time. Over 2000 years have passed, and most, or over 90% of the ramparts of the capital, have disappeared.

Not far away from the ancient graves, people found some relics of workshops producing pottery, bronze ware and jade articles. They also found molds for producing coins: Dao coins of Zhao State, Bu coins of Yan State, and Chengbai coins of Zhongshan State.

Chen Yingqi:
The relic site of the workshops is not far away from the relic site of ancient graves. Since we research on relic sites of ancient cities, we have some experience on this. We believe that the relic site is inside the ancient capital.

The discovery of a large number of relic sites of workshops and residences as well as scattered cultural relics was a good start

The Mysterious Zhongshan State

Molds for Producing Coins

The Relic Site of the Workshops

Chen Yingqi
Researcher with Hebei Province Cultural Relics Research Institute

Pilasters and rock pillar bases are in good order on the ground.

Liu Laicheng
Researcher with Hebei Province Cultural Relics Research Institute

The tiles are not common ones. They are big tiles used to build palace. From these tiles, we can tell that the grave is a king's grave.

According to the ancient funeral system of China, the commemorative architecture above the ground is an important component of kings' graves. The architecture on the earth heap is called "Xiang Hall". Although the Xiang Hall collapsed in the rains and storms of the past two thousand years, we can still tell from the drawing made by archaeological architects after measurement of the relics that, the architecture above the grave is composed of one layer of Xiang Hall and two layers of cloisters. It is grand and towering, and indicates the distinctive status of the owner of the grave.

Chen Yingqi:

We drilled to find a passage like a Chinese character Zhong (or center) "中". The passage can be divided into a south passage and a north passage, and there is a coffin chamber in the middle. According to the ancient system, this is a king's grave.

for us to make clear the relation between the ancient graves and the capital of the Zhongshan State. Meanwhile, a more in-depth archaeological excavation action had started with Grave SN1.

Grave SN1 is the largest in size among the graves. After more than two thousand years of rains and storms, the earth heap over the grave mound is still 15m high, and its baseline is 92m long from east to west, and 110m long from south to north. The surface of the heap is basically square. There are three steps, and the architectural relics still remain on the second step.

By expanding the scope of the excavation, people found six accompanying graves,

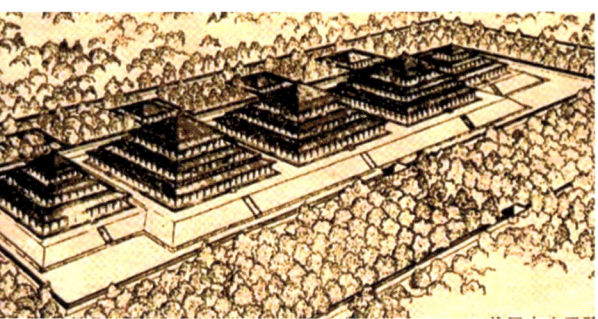

The Model on the Grave Made by Archaeological Architects

one horse-and-chariot pit, and one burial article pit around Grave SN1. Although the graves and pits have been severely robbed, there are still abundant cultural relics in them.

Chen Yingqi
Researcher with Hebei Province Cultural Relics Research Institute

Particularly, the No.2 accompanying grave on the east side of Grave SN1 is totally filled with white sand of about seven or eight meters thick. It is complete and has not been robbed.

The persons were buried with their heads pointing to Grave SN1. This indicates that they were closely related to the owner of Grave SN1, and should be wives and concubines of the owner.

Chen Yingqi:
The bones of the person buried in the central grave were rotten. However, the three rows of jade plates he wore were completely in good condition.

From the relics in the unearthed accompanying graves, we can tell the status of the owners. Most relics unearthed from the five accompanying graves are black potteries, jade articles and bronze ware. All these things have good decorating effects but poor value in use. Apparently, they were made to be buried and not the articles the dead used when they were alive. Compression and polishing techniques were applied to the surfaces of the unfired potteries. As a result, the decorative patterns of the black potteries are a shiny, lustrous black, but the backgrounds are a flat, opaque black. So these black potteries look elegant.

People also unearthed a large number of jade articles. There are flat jade rings for rites, jade plates for decoration, jade combs and hooks, jade figures and some jade toys. They are all excellent jade works, and reflect the honorable status of the owner. This eddy-grain flat jade ring is quite symmetric, gentle and pure. After a long caress by its owner, it looks extraordinarily fine and smooth.

What people unearthed from the No.6 accompanying grave, which is farther, are mostly some rough gray potteries and small jade articles.

Ying had disappeared from the marriage system in the Period of Warring States. Therefore, the owner of the No.6 grave must be a woman slave. A man who had a group of wives and concubines must have a larger group of woman slaves. How come only she was buried beside the master? This is a mystery.

Two sets of dog bones were unearthed from the burial article pit. On the necks of the dogs there were rings made of gold. When unearthed, the rings still shone.

What is most noticeable is the boat pit, which is very rare among the ancient graves in North China. The surface plane of the boat pit is like the Chinese character Tu"凸", and the channel in the north symbolizes a riverway. When the boat pit is opened, the wooden boat had already rotten completely. However, the ash relics as well as the serial bells and musical stones in the cabin remain as if to re-create the sights and sounds that the master saw and listened to: the sound of the metals and stones, the beautiful dances, and the view from a boat on the Hutuo River.

In the winter of 1974, heavy snow covered the fields of North China. The archaeologists completed the excavation of Grave SN1, the accompanying graves, and the burial article pit. An important achievement of the excavation is that the status of the owner of the major grave was confirmed to be a king. However, the excavation of the main grave was not planned.

Liu Laicheng
Researcher with Hebei Province Cultural Relics Research Institute

Why did we stop excavation? There are probably very important relics in the largest grave. We didn't dare to start excavation of it carelessly, and we were afraid of damage to the relics. We have to be careful. Although the relics on the ground and in the accompanying graves had been cleaned up, we hadn't fully understood everything around.

However, the field investigation of Lingshou, capital of the Zhongshan State was not affected by the heavy snow.

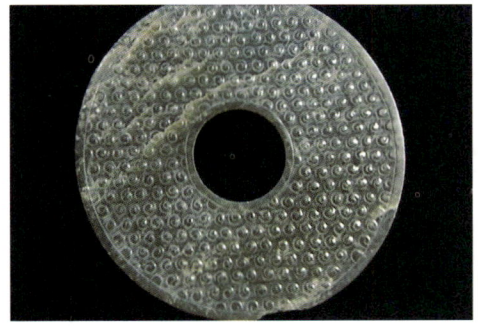

The Eddy-grain Flat Jade Ring

The Black Pottery

Chinese Archaeological Discoveries

The Excavation Spot of the Boat Pit

Chen Yingqi
Researcher with Hebei Province Cultural Relics Research Institute

We rescued the relics in the heavy snow. The peasants didn't stop, and we continued working too.

Not far away from the group of ancient graves, people found the rammed ground of a section of ancient rampart. In an investigation of greater scope, the archaeologists found more and more similar rampart relics. This is not a completely accidental phenomenon. If we connect the different sections of ramparts, we see an ancient city. This is an old city at the foot of mountains and beside rivers. The shape of the city is like an irregular pear. It is approximately 4km from east to west and 4.5km from south to north. The whole city zone can be divided into two parts. In the eastern part, the palace area is in the north and the residential area is in the south. In the western part, the bazaar area is in the south, the workshop area in the middle, and kings' grave area in the north. In the city, people also found an even more important piece of evidence.

Chen Yingqi:
There is a small hill in Zhongshan State. Behind the hill, there are still rammed ramparts as well as foundations of the ramparts.

This discovery completely agrees with the historical record: "Zhongshan

The Recovery Drawing of the Ancient City

The Mysterious Zhongshan State

The Relic Site of Grave SN6

people's custom was to enclose the hill in the town". Enclosing the hill in the town was a custom of the Zhongshan people. This indicates that the Zhongshan people still worshipped mountains after leaving the high mountains.

In the autumn of 1975, the archaeologists started excavating Grave SN6. Although it is smaller than Grave SN1, its passage is up to 90m long. Unfortunately, the major coffin chamber of Grave SN6 had been heavily robbed, and nothing was left.

Chen Yingqi
Researcher with Hebei Province Cultural Relics Research Institute
The outer coffin was robbed and collapsed. The wooden plate on the outer coffin collapsed, and the rammed earth fell.

When people began to lose their hope, one incident made a favorable turn in the excavation.

Chen Yingqi:
We excavated. A peasant laborer stepped on the earth. All of a sudden, he stepped into a hole, a big hole. He was scared. Heavy smoke rose from the hole. People pulled him out of the hole. The smoke was actually steam.

Nobody had expected that a treasure house be found on the side of the major coffin chamber when the peasant laborer walked there.

Chen Yingqi:
The person on duty was found. He took a flashlight with him to the hole, and saw that inside the hole was collapsed earth.

The Bronze Ware with the Shape of a Chinese Character "山"

183

A burial pattern, which had never been found in the archaeological excavation before, appeared. On both sides of the coffin chamber, there are two warehouses for storing burial articles, and they are not connected to the major coffin chamber.

Chen Yingqi
Researcher with Hebei Province Cultural Relics Research Institute

Unexpected, really unexpected. We thought this was just an empty grave. We didn't expect two warehouses. We didn't expect these gains.

The later excavations proved that this unconventional design of the coffin chamber structure was a unique feature of the graves of Zhongshan kings. It was because of this feature that most treasures in the graves of Zhongshan kings escaped from the repeated robberies of the past 2000 odd years. From the warehouses on both sides of the major coffin chamber, several hundred cultural relics were unearthed, and a large number of them are rare treasures.

The Silver-head Servant Bronze Lamp

The most unique ones are the bronze ware whose shape is like a Chinese character "山". They are 143cm high, and weigh over 50kg. There are six of them. Similar bronze ware had never been unearthed in the archaeological excavations of the Period of Warring States relics before. People had different ideas about its use.

Liu Laicheng
Researcher with Hebei Province Cultural Relics Research Institute

We think the bronze ware was an emblem of the Zhongshan State, but some people believe it was a decoration on a flagpole. Actually it was too big to be a decoration on a flagpole, as nobody could hold the flagpole. However, they have their own reasons for saying it was a decoration on a flagpole.

Today, people have been aware that this special and grand bronze ware carried the spirit of the ancient Xianyu people, and the embodiment of the national will of the Zhongshan State. It was a national emblem.

Out of the unearthed cultural relics, there are nine attractive three-legged bronze tripots. In ancient China, tripots were sovereign ritual articles. In Western Zhou, only the Son of Heaven was entitled to use nine tripots. Therefore, the discovery of nine tripots in the grave of the Zhongshan king proves the "breakdown of rites and deterioration of music" in the society under the rule of the Son of

Heaven in the Spring and Autumn Period as well as in the Period of Warring States. It also proves that Xianyu people, while maintaining some clan customs after moving to the agricultural area, had started to imitate the rites of the powerful states and their lifestyles became more Han-like. They stepped onto the stage of the Warring States Period with a brand new look.

A typical article is the silver-head servant bronze lamp. The servant wears Han-style clothes, which are characterized by broad sleeves, oblique collar, and an opening on the right side. These clothes are totally different from the narrow-sleeved clothes and long-gowns the Xianyu people wore before. The hairstyle of the servant also changes from the ox horn style to this one.

"Men play games together, singing songs munificently; women play musical instruments, pleasing the rich and the noble." This is a historical record about the Zhongshan State. This young man radiant with smiles lets us enjoy this echo from over 2000 years ago.

After over two years of preparations, they started excavation of Grave No. 1

Chen Yingqi
Researcher with Hebei Province Cultural Relics Research Institute

We drilled first. When we reached 10 odd meters, the drill fell into the hole. We couldn't pull it out, so we had to wait until we excavated the grave.

The hole the archaeologists drilled led to a treasure house similar to those of Grave No.6. In-depth excavation proves that Grave No.1 is very similar to Grave No.6 in structure. The only difference is an additional treasure house on the northeast of the major coffin chamber of Grave No.1. That means they would find more relics in Grave No.1, and the status of this king is higher.

The following discovery was both expected and unexpected. A robber's hole was found on the north of the high earth heap, obliquely cutting into the coffin chamber.

Chen Yingqi:

What did we find in the robber's hole? We think the Zhongshan king called Cuo wore a leather coat. The robber got the coat and crept through the hole. The diameter of the hole is just one odd meter, and there are several stones the robber threw from the chamber into the hole. When the robber crept in the hole, some of the bronze adornments on the leather coat were hooked on the stone and fell off. Also, we found several silver coins. They looked like seashells, so we call them silver shells.

Everything told them that they wouldn't get anything from the chamber. When the earth heap was removed, what happened with this robber's hole could be deduced. The robbery that took place in the late Period of Warring States left nothing in the largest coffin chamber but several big bronze rings for suspending the coffin and some damaged relics. And after the robbery, the robber set fire to the chamber, and everything was burnt.

However, nobody noticed one rare treasure in a corner of the chamber, which the robber missed. It was under the stones. People would find it later, as at that time, they all focused their attention on the three treasure houses.

Chen Yingqi
Researcher with Hebei Province Cultural Relics Research Institute

What was found first was a double-winged supernatural beast, which was upside down. One of our comrades used a bamboo prod to slowly clear the earth. The claws of the beast pointed upward, and lacerated his hand. He said to me: Master Chen, what is this pointed stuff. I looked at it, and told him to continue clearing carefully.

The silver double-winged supernatural beast looks like the wind god "Fei Lian" of ancient Chinese myth, with its wide-open eyes, shrieking, open mouth, and its sharp crisscrossed teeth. With chest broad and low and buttocks slightly upward, it seems ready to take off at any time. On the surface of the beast, silver plates and threads make varied spotted marks, with which the beast looks powerful, lifelike and mysterious.

Among the large amount of beautiful relics unearthed from Grave SN1, there are bells, tripots, serial musical stones, and bronze ware symbolizing kingship as well as a musical and ritual system, and

The Silver Double-winged Supernatural Beast

The Mysterious Zhongshan State

there are also many beautiful and delicate household goods.

Gold- and silver-inlaid four-dragon and four-phoenix square table seat. The principal part is the dragons and phoenixes. The four divine dragons, with front claws as support and heads and tails extending in each direction, stand firm on a round plate supported by four crouching deer. The whole design breaks through the old-fashioned design measures taken in Shang Dynasty and Zhou Dynasty. It is so novel and delicate, and is an extremely rare treasure.

Gold- and silver-inlaid tiger biting deer. It is the base of a folding screen. A martial tiger with a colorful and vigorous body bends its body, turns its head to the right, waves its tail like a steel scourge, and bites into a deer it just catches. The valor and celerity of the tiger and the weakness and helplessness of the deer make a vivid contrast, and forms a lifelike picture of the law of the jungle. Another folding screen base is gold- and silver-inlaid bronze cattle. The cattle looks tame and calm. The animals are all inlaid with gold and silver. The brightness of the gold and silver enhance the artistic charm of the articles.

Bronze lamp. In ancient China, bronzes lamps were both household goods and works of art. The fifteen connected lamps unearthed from Grave SN1 are the best

Gold- and Silver-inlaid Four-dragon and Four-phoenix Square Table Seat

The Fifteen Connected Lamps

among all existing bronze lamps. The overall structure looks like a big tree. The trunk of the tree is supported by three tigers, and the fifteen lamps are on the branches. On the branches, there are also swimming dragons, chirping birds, as well as playing monkeys. Some of the monkeys hang onto the tree by one arm, and some jump from one branch to another. There are also two persons playing with the monkeys under the tree. We had repeatedly unearthed connected lamps from the graves of Period of Warring States before, but we had rarely seen such connected lamps with so many animals and persons.

As beautiful relics were unearthed one after another, the excavation seemed to reach its peak. However, the archaeologists were not satisfied at all.

Chen Yingqi
Researcher with Hebei Province Cultural Relics Research Institute

These relics did belong to Zhongshan State. They have the style of Zhongshan State, not the style of Yan State or Zhao State. However, we didn't find the Chinese characters of "Zhongshan" to confirm it.

Before paper was invented, Chinese people used bamboo slips and hardware to carry Chinese characters. To completely uncover the mystery of the Zhongshan State, we need the most precious evidence, Chinese characters. People were waiting anxiously.

Liu Laicheng
Researcher with Hebei Province Cultural Relics Research Institute

I was thinking, how great it would be if we could unearth big tripots inscribed with Chinese characters!

When the treasure house on the east was cleaned up, people opened the treasure house on the northeast. To everyone's surprise, the house was empty. They didn't find any trace of robbery, or burial articles.

Chen Yingqi:

We didn't know why. People surmised that the house might be used to hold clothes and silk cloth. We didn't see anything because the clothes and cloth were totally rotten. Anyway, we didn't see anything even when we cleaned to the bottom. It was really a pity.

The Gold-and Silver-inlaid Tiger Biting Deer

Fortunately, many relics were unearthed from the treasure house on the west, which made up for the disappointment to some extent. Over two years of excavation, more than 19,000 cultural relics were unearthed. These delicate and wonderful articles are totally different from the cultural relics of the Warring States Period unearthed from other places. They change the artistic style of Shang Dynasty and Zhou Dynasty, which is characterized by mystery and seriousness, and show us rich imaginations and positive vigor. Through them, one can see the local conditions and customs of the Zhongshan State, and become closer to the state that had disappeared over 2000 years ago.

The end of the excavation was approaching, and people had butterflies in their stomachs. It was another dusk.

Liu Laicheng
Researcher with Hebei Province Cultural Relics Research Institute

We took a lot of jade articles from the treasure house on the west. I wondered if we could get any article with Chinese characters. Fortunately, we found an article with Chinese characters. It was a square flagon.

I bent to look at the flagon. Heavens! I found a lot of characters. I told them to take the flagon out. We found a lot of Chinese characters on each side of the flagon. I told people to report to Shijiazhuang as soon as possible. It was so great. The big stuff had many Chinese characters on each side.

People wondered what the characters on the heavy bronze ware told us.

Chen Yingqi
Researcher with Hebei Province Cultural Relics Research Institute

Our comrades cleaned the flagon. They used bamboo prods to remove the earth and rust from the flagon. Three characters appeared before us: Zhong Shan King.

Looking at the three clear Chinese characters, people couldn't help cheering. The big flagon, which is 63cm tall and weighs 28kg, has an inscription of 450 Chinese characters on four sides. The inscription tells us that the greatest king of the Zhongshan State, "Cuo", is buried here. The inscription also tells us something about the war against the Yan State. In

The Bronze Square Flagon with Chinese Characters

314 BC, when the Yan State suffered from civil strife aroused by defence against the Qi State, the Zhongshan king Cuo breached the agreement with the Yan State, and ordered his forces to attack the Yan State from three directions. He occupies a large territory from Yan State. This big bronze ware was made to commemorate the victory in the war against the Yan State, and the material used to make this flagon was taken from the defeated state. "Ancestors Wen, Wu, Huan and Cheng" in the inscription indicates that there were four kings before Cuo: King Wen, King Wu, King Huan and King Cheng. The owner of Grave SN6 was King Cheng, the fourth king of the Zhongshan State. King Cuo in Grave SN1 was the fifth king of Zhongshan State.

The Round Bronze Flagon

In terms of both dimension and quality, the nine bronze tripots unearthed from Grave SN1 are much better than the nine tripots unearthed from King Cheng's grave. The largest iron-leg bronze tripot

The Ancient Chinese Characters on the Big Flagon

has a 469-character inscription. This is the longest inscription among all bronze wares of the period of Warring States. Another round bronze flagon has a 204-character inscription. These inscriptions also give description of the war against the Yan State.

The three bronze wares provide extremely precious historical data for researching the history of the Zhongshan State, and represent the most advanced technology in the period of Warring States. The characters of the inscriptions are beautiful and smooth. This indicates that the Zhongshan State, after the rejuvenation and the rule of King Huan and King Cheng, started to combine its culture with Han culture under the rule of Cuo.

The Zhongshan State under the rule of Cuo gradually grew into "a state of a thousand chariots". The chariot Cuo rode was remarkably decorated. The gold parts and the gold and silver ornaments shining after more than two thousand years display the ambition of the Zhongshan king. Two years after the victory of the war against the Yan State, Cuo fell ill and failed to recover. He died soon after. In 313 BC, funeral music and paper made to resemble money was everywhere in Lingshou. The whole state held a ceremonious funeral for him. On the bronze flagon buried with Cuo, the inscription warns people that "you should not run wild when you are strong; you should not be too proud when you are rich; you should not be arrogant when you enjoy many helpful hands. Your personal enemies are around you, and you can not run away from your inexorable doom."

In 1977 when 2291 years had passed, a trip to the mysterious Zhongshan State was coming to an end. People were unmindfully doing their final work. At this moment, a staff moved a stone in the corner by chance, only to find a large twisted bronze plate!

Liu Laicheng
Researcher with Hebei Province Cultural Relics Research Institute
At first we didn't attach importance to this stuff. It was just a bronze plate.

The Iron-Leg Bronze Tripot

This quadrate bronze plate was burnt and twisted in the fire the robber set.

Liu Laicheng
Researcher with Hebei Province Cultural Relics Research Institute

The plate melted a little bit in the fire, and wood ash and stones fell on the plate, sticking to it.

After the clean-up, people were surprised to find that this 96cm-long and 48cm-wide bronze plate had a layout made

A Construction Plan Made of Gold and Silver Threads on the Bronze Plate

of gold and silver threads, and beside the layout were remarks. What is this layout?

Chen Yingqi
Researcher with Hebei Province Cultural Relics Research Institute

It is a construction plan, which is unparalleled in the world. It is also the only plan of an ancient king's grave in China.

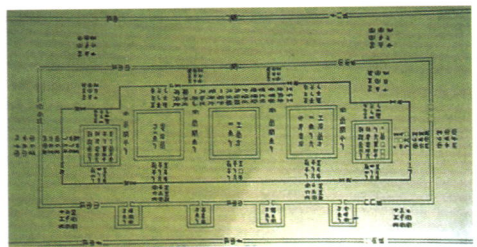

The Ancient Construction Plan Depicted by Archaeologists

The Excavation Site of Grave SN1

The Mysterious Zhongshan State

The Reduplicative Chariots

The Gold Components of the Chariots

The kings and emperors of all dynasties wanted to be immortal by creating impressive achievements. According to the plan, King Cuo's grave architecture was magnificent. In the middle is "Xiang Hall" of Cuo; on both sides were two Queen's Halls; the whole grave area was divided into an internal palace and an external palace. However, the plan wasn't realized except for Xiang Hall on top of the grave.

When King Cuo died, Zhao State that had been feuding with the Zhongshan State was implementing "the movement of wearing Hu-style clothes, riding horses and shooting arrows" and carrying out policies for making the state rich and building up its military power. In the Zhongshan State, the soldiers were neglectful about their weapons; the peasants were lazy about farming; the politics were decadent; and the people were demoralized. The scout of King Wuling of Zhao State looked around in the Zhongshan State and returned to report that the Zhongshan State was doomed to perish.

In 296 BC, when the cavalries of Zhao State marched toward the Zhongshan State, the sixth king of Zhongshan State, who vowed solemnly to rejuvenate his state, ran away to another state, and eventually died there. At that time, Cuo's wife, who was still alive, was exiled. As the queen of the former king left, the state that had played such an important role in history disappeared. Its subjects spread to a broader land, while the state and its history were buried underground, and weren't found until 2270 years later.

On January 13, 1988, the relic site of the capital city of Zhongshan State was granted governmental protection as a historical and cultural site. In Sanji Town of Pingshan County, where the relic site is located, there are currently 15 administrative villages and 20,000 villagers.

The Emperor's Burial Objects

In May 1990, the archaeologists in Shaanxi were carefully cleaning up an ancient pit. The thousand-year-old dirt was removed bit by bit and the hidden secret was about to come to light in the 20th century.

The first sight of the pit was puzzling. When the archaeologists removed the dirt, there appeared a head of a pottery figurine. By its side, there were many broken limbs and heads of pottery figurines. The facial expressions of the figurines were very diverse: some of them were smiling, others meditating. They reminded us of the famous terracotta soldiers and horses in Qinshihuang's Mausoleum, but they looked quite different. Who are they? And why were they left here?

The Emperor's Burial Objects

CHINESE ARCHAEOLOGICAL DISCOVERIES

The Xianyang International Airport of Xi'an is one of the busiest airports in China. To every tourist in China, the second destination, next to the capital city of Beijing, is usually Xi'an. The fame of the city lies in her long history. Xi'an used to be the capital of 11 dynasties. Therefore, many historical and cultural relics of various times have been preserved here, including the world-famous terracotta soldiers and horses.

Not far away from the Xianyang International Airport, people discovered that on the northern side of the freeway, there stood two strange hillocks. They were especially conspicuous on the boundless fields. Anyone with an inkling of archaeological knowledge would realize that they must be the mounds of ancient mausoleums and that an eminent personage must have been buried underneath.

The modern freeway runs across the fields, but it cannot penetrate history.

To the villagers that have lived here for generations, those hillocks that appeared so puzzling to outsiders were no secret at all. Almost everyone here knows that the place where they live is a mausoleum of a Chinese emperor from over 2000 years ago. It was named "Yang Ling Mausoleum," and the emperor and empress were buried beneath the hillocks.

To the ancient people, the grand mausoleums were symbols of power and wealth. However to modern people, these mounds mean a mysterious underground world and strange ancient times.

One day in 1972, the administration of cultural relics of Shaanxi received an urgent task. The officials were ordered to make haste to Yang Ling Mausoleum. It was said that the villagers nearby discovered human remains when constructing irrigation works.

On the spot, the archaeologists excavated

The Emperor's Burial Objects

35 human skeletons. After the excavation, the skeletons were re-buried in the earth. What was preserved in the Archaeological Museum of Yang Ling Mausoleum of Han were some iron wares excavated at that time. They were ancient instruments of torture used in the confinement of the criminals. According to history, ancient Chinese emperors often ordered criminals to build mausoleums. It is likely that these poor souls were the criminals that built the Yang Ling Mausoleum.

Here is the criminals' burial ground. It is located over 1000 meters northwest of the imperial mausoleum. To everyone's amazement, over 10,000 people's remains were buried in this area of 80,000 square meters. It was inferred that they died of heavy labor, diseases, or accidents in the construction of the mausoleum.

Nearly 40 km away from the Yang Ling Mausoleum, there stands one of the greatest projects in human history, that is, Qinshihuang's Mausoleum. It is recorded that in 38 years, Emperor Qinshihuang ordered more than 700,000 people to build his mausoleum and treated those who served him with the cruelest laws. His abuse of the people's resources ended up with the collapse of his empire.

Only four years after Emperor Qinshihuang's death, the once-powerful empire of Qin perished. In 202 BC, the empire of the Western Han once more united China.

The Yang Ling Mausoleum

The Yang Ling Mausoleum was built at the beginning of the Western Han dynasty. It was just one century later than Qinshihuang's Mausoleum, but its scale could not be compared to that of Qinshihuang's Mausoleum. However, after so many years, the mounds of the imperial mausoleum remain as high as 32 meters. Such a project is almost impossible for over 2000 years ago.

Jiao Nanfeng

Director of the Shaanxi Archaeological Institute

The mounds of the imperial mausoleum are 300,000 cubic meters in volume. According to the conditions back then, if every worker carried and rammed one cubic meter of earth per day, the project would need 300,000 workers. In fact, the labor force at that time could not have had such work efficiency.

No one can estimate the exact number of the people who used to work here. To modern people, this emperor is just as cruel and tyrannical as Emperor Qinshihuang, as both of them sacrificed so many lives for their afterlives. However, in the historical records of ancient China, the master of the Yang Ling Mausoleum was one of the most famous benevolent emperors.

His name is Liu Qi. He is the 4th emperor of the empire of Western Han. His reign lasted 16 years. After his death, people respectfully called him Emperor Jing, which means that he had strong determination and will power to promote kind-heartedness and justice.

At that time in China, cruelty to criminals would not affect an emperor's achievements. Thanks to his kind-heartedness to the majority of the subjects and ministers, Emperor Jing won unanimous acclaim from ancient historians.

People nowadays are very interested in the resting place of Emperor Jing. However, in order to better protect the underground relics, Chinese archaeologists usually only carry out tentative explorations to large-scale imperial mausoleums and make no haste to excavate. After the discovery of the criminals' burial ground of the Yang Ling Mausoleum, the area soon resumed its former tranquility. It was not until 18 years later that a special event took place.

In the spring of 1990, the municipal government of Xi'an decided to build a freeway to the airport to provide better traffic facilities for tourists. The route of the freeway passed through the Yang Ling Mausoleum. Therefore, an archaeological team was first sent to the construction site to carry out tentative archaeological explorations.

The Emperor's Burial Objects

The Relic Site of Attendant Burial Graves in the Yang Ling Mausoleum

Mr. Wang Baoping has been engaged in archaeology since he was 18 years old. A large part of his archaeological life has been spent in the Yang Ling Mausoleum. He has covered almost every inch of the Yang Ling area.

Wang Baoping

Vice Curator of the Archaeological Museum of Yang Ling Mausoleum of Han

I wore pants and a vest the other day in the maize field. I worked from 8 am to 3 pm with a few workers. The sun was very hot, and the maize leaves rubbed my arms red. Why did I do that? I had got some sense. I had new discoveries.

Right beneath the roadbed of the planned freeway, indeed there were some underground pits.

After the explorations, people discovered that the underground pits in the Yang Ling Mausoleum were very large in scale. In the two areas that were first verified, there were altogether 48 pits. Archaeologists judged that they were attendant burial graves in the Yang Ling Mausoleum.

Chinese Archaeological Discoveries

The Relic Site of Attendant Burial Graves

Wang Xueli

Research fellow of the Shaanxi Archaeological Institute

I think the relation between the pits and mausoleum is as between master and attendant. The host of the mausoleum is the master, and the objects buried on the outskirts were attendants buried following the master. So I call those pits "attendant burial graves".

In ancient China, only emperors, the feudal princes, and high-ranking officials were entitled to arrange attendant burial graves beside the main mausoleum. Usually, the graves hold very deep symbolic meaning. The terracotta pits in Qinshihuang's Mausoleum are attendant burial graves.

The first group of attendant burial graves in the Yang Ling Mausoleum was divided into the southern and northern sections. They keep a distance from the imperial mausoleum and form a relatively independent system. The southern section is located 300 meters south of the empress' mausoleum and consists of 24 pits. The northern section is situated on the northwest, 500 meters away from the emperor's mausoleum and consists also of 24 pits. Archaeologists numbered these pits respectively.

These pits were arranged in regular order and represented certain manners in the emperor's lifetime. However, what exactly do they represent?

In order not to interrupt the road construction, the archaeological team carried out excavations to the No.6, No.8, No.17, and No.24 pits in the southern section. Among them, the No. 8 pit is 291 meters long, which is 81 meters longer than the famous No.1 terracotta pit in Qinshihuang's Mausoleum.

Not long after breaking through the modern farming soil, archaeologists discovered terrible holes by tomb-robbers.

The Emperor's Burial Objects

Would nothing but disappointment be awaiting the archaeologists?

Luckily, in the underground pits, there were some objects in which the robbers took no interest. The first objects that attracted people's attention were the heads of the pottery figurines scattered in the soil. Beside them, there were also many piles of pottery limbs.

The broken pottery figurines were carried out of the pits and sent to the repair workshop for cultural relics. There was controversy among archaeologists themselves concerning their images. The pottery figurines unearthed in the past usually had complete clothes inscribed on their bodies, whereas figurines like these were unprecedented. After careful cleaning, collating and repairs, these 2000-year-old pottery figurines were again exposed to people's sight.

The Excavation Spot of the Southern Section of the Attendant Burial Grave

The scale of the figurines is only one third the size of real people. They are about 60 cm high and every figurine is naked and painted orange. All the organs on their bodies, including genitals and bellybuttons, were carefully and faithfully inscribed. What is strange is that all the figurines are armless.

Therefore, some call them "Oriental Venuses."

Why are they like this?

After the clearage of the four underground pits, they were refilled and leveled up. The newly built freeway runs on top of them. Every day there are innumerable people who pass this road, but few of them know that in the very place they pass in haste lies the history of over 2000 years ago and many puzzles that are waiting to be solved.

The construction of the freeway brought about opportunities to the Yang Ling Mausoleum. The Archaeological Team of Yang Ling Mausoleum has hence set out to work. After the clearage and refiling work of the attendant burial graves under the roadbed of the freeway, the Archaeological Team began all-round explorations and excavations.

While excavating the No.20 pit in the southern section, people met with a surprising spectacle. At the bottom of a

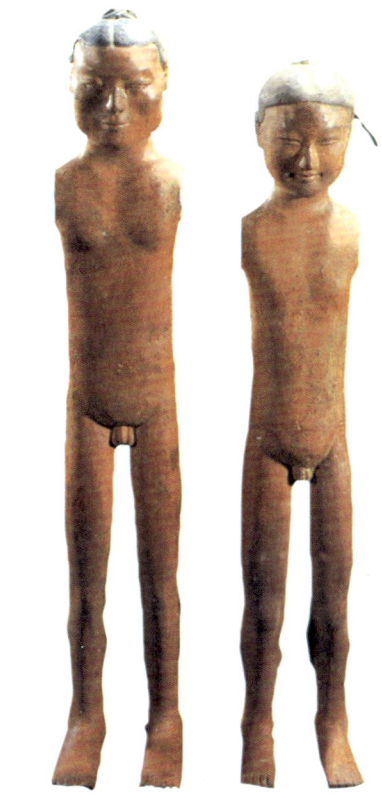

Naked Male Figurines

hole, there lay a body. Judging from the two bricks beside it, it was supposed that he was one of the tomb robbers. When he was standing in the pit and passing the treasures to his accomplice, the accomplice killed him out of greed.

Despite the robbery, there were still a variety of cultural relics in this pit. In between the planks filled with earth, hundreds of pottery warrior figurines were placed in good order.

The Emperor's Burial Objects

Wang Baoping
Vice Curator of the Archaeological Museum of Yang Ling Mausoleum of Han

We were very excited. We unearthed so many warrior figurines buried over 2000 years ago and they represent the powerful and brave soldiers of the Han dynasty.

Besides the complete body apertures, there is also a complete set of small body parts. Everything is very small, refined, and made with extreme care. Everything is complete.

The Pottery Figurines with Traces of Armaments or Clothes

On the surface of some pottery figurines unearthed this time, people discovered traces of armaments or clothes. With the confirmation of the real objects, people finally made clear of the origin of the naked figurines.

It turns out that at the completion of the project, all the figurines were wearing beautiful clothes made of fine silk or normal sackcloth. The round holes on their shoulders were for fixing wooden arms. In this way, the arms of the figurines could turn as freely as those of modern dolls. However with the lapse of time, the clothes and wood rotted away. Therefore, only the naked armless bodies remained. These figurines used to wear colorful outfits and majestic armaments. They also had small iron weapons in hand and the cavalrymen also had fine wooden horses under them. The expression of every figurine is different.

To people's surprise, in the troops of

Pottery Warrior Figurines

warriors, there stood some healthy and beautiful women, some of whom were even in cavalries. Most of them have delicate features and symmetrical builds.

Strangely, there are also several women soldiers among them that are extremely ugly, their faces spoiled with the high cheekbones. Were there indeed women like these? Some inferred that they perhaps belonged to some minor ethnic groups in faraway areas and thus looked quite different from the others.

The Ugly-looking Pottery Figurine

The Painted Female Pottery Figurines

In tomb robbers' eyes, these clay-made figurines could not be compared with the splendid gold, silver and jade wares and were thrown away. But in fact, back in the Han dynasty, these naked pottery figurines could only be in the emperors' possession and represented the highest standards. After thousands of years, these figurines have become invaluable treasures in modern people's minds.

Tourist from the UK:
It's absolutely fascinating. It really is a wonderful experience to be here.

These pottery figurines have preserved forever the ancient people's image. They have enabled us to face our ancestors to this day, share their sorrow and joy, and imagine their life stories.

It is said in ancient Chinese legends that in remote antiquity there was an ancestor named Nü Wa. She made many small human figures with earth according to her own looks and endowed them with life. Hence humans came into being.

In the Chinese ancients' beliefs, earth is sacred. Life comes from earth and shall return to earth in the end.

Earth is the foundation of agricultural civilization. The yellow earth not only cultivated abundant food, but also brought boundless creativity to people. Among all the ancient nations in the world, the Chinese were perhaps the best in their usage of earth. They made use of the molding capabilities of yellow earth and fired various exquisite ceramics and variform pottery figurines.

They came from the rich and profound land. Through craftsmen's skillful hands and the baking of the blazing fire, the

The Emperor's Burial Objects

image of life gradually emerged out of earth.

Among the ancient Chinese pottery figurines unearthed up to now, the most well-known ones are the terracotta soldiers and horses in Qinshihuang's Mausoleum. The troops represent the great army that served the emperor in his lifetime. All the soldiers and horses are as tall and gigantic as real ones. The soldiers have complete suits of armor. They look very solemn and ready to fight a fierce battle at any time.

Like the terracotta soldiers and horses in Qinshihuang's Mausoleum, most of the buried figurines in the 48 attendant burial graves in the Yang Ling Mausoleum were warriors. Therefore, they have been identified to be the imperial army.

Jiao Nanfeng
Director of the Shaanxi Archaeological Institute

In military terms, the emperor of the Han dynasty abolished all feudal princes from the local army. Besides the frontier defense army, the main military force, the so-called field army in modern terms, was divided into the southern and northern troops. The mission of the southern troops was to guard the imperial palace, whereas that of the northern troop was to protect Chang'an City and resist the invasion of northern ethnic groups. So some experts think that the southern attendant burial graves represent the southern troops and the northern ones represent the northern troop of the Han dynasty.

Compared with the terracotta soldiers and horses, Emperor Jing's warriors are much shorter. They are also less strong and solemn. Although they are warriors, their airs are anything but grave and solemn. Their preparations for the war are more like some elegant dance.

These figurines' faces are flowing with liveliness. Some of them are melancholy, others calm, and still others happy. On these figurines, human nature is vividly and richly portrayed. Their faces are without traces of affliction from warfare and cruel laws. The soldiers are relaxed and natural in spirit.

All these have formed a sharp contrast with the terracotta soldiers. This is a symbol of the general peace and tranquility of the Emperor Jing's reign.

The first several emperors of the Han Empire learned a lesson from the perdition of the Qin dynasty and adopted the rehabilitation policy of inflicting little labor and tax on people. Especially during the reigns of Emperor Jing and his father Emperor Wen, the empire enjoyed general peace and tranquility. People called this precious period the "Great Order of Wen and Jing." The scores of years of benevolent policy accumulated treasure and power for the formerly weak empire of the Western Han, which later became a strong empire that dominated East Asia.

Today, all tourists to Xi'an would visit the well-preserved ancient ramparts, which is one of the most attractive scenic spots in China. However, not many people know that in fact, these bricks have only a history of over 600 years, whereas the ancient thousand-year-long capital is located northwest of the ramparts.

In 202 BC, Liu Bang, the first emperor of the Western Han dynasty built the new capital on the southern bank of the Weihe River and named it Chang'an, meaning "peaceful forever." Hundreds of years later, Chang'an became the capital of the Tang dynasty. In the 9th century AD, the prosperity of the city came to its peak and the capital was one of the biggest and greatest in the world at that time.

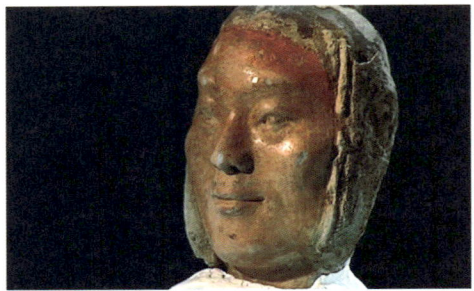

The Figurine's Face with Liveliness

Nowadays, the above-ground remnants of the ancient Chang'an city are scarce. The results of archaeological excavation can only vaguely describe the former contours of the ancient capital.

This deserted huge heap of earth used to bear the weight of a grand and splendid

The Ancient City of Xi'an

The Emperor's Burial Objects

palace named "Wei Yang Palace" from over 2000 years ago. It was the emperors' residence in the Western Han period and Emperor Jing once lived here.

What was the emperor's palace like? What treasures were hidden in it? These questions are hard to answer. The lapse of time has changed the geographical features. In the face of nothing but this mound, it hardly supplies anything to feed our imaginations.

However, the mysterious underground mausoleums usually can preserve part of the remote past. The underground palace hidden under the mound probably represented the emperor's imperial sleeping palace. If the palace were not destroyed, perhaps we would have been privileged to witness the legendary ancient palace and the emperor that once ruled China.

Wang Xueli
Research fellow of the Shaanxi Archaeological Institute

I should say that the basic shape of the underground palace is still there. But I'm not clear about the layout of Emperor Jing's mausoleum, since it has not been excavated. But what we do know is that according to history , the insurrectionist army used to dig open all the Han mausoleums after they fought their way to the central Shaanxi plain at the end of the Western Han period. They did it out of revenge.

For over 2000 years, nature did not destroy the work of human toil, however, historical misfortunes brought about more disasters. The underground palace under the mound has perhaps been entirely different. What spectacle will it present? There is no answer to this puzzle for the time being.

Luckily, near the imperial mound, the Archaeological Team found another 90 radially distributed pits. They are attendant burial graves of the main mausoleum as well. However, these graves are different from those of troops on the outskirts. They are near the imperial mausoleum, and some of them even overlap under the mounds. The indication is very clear. They represent the organization and furnishings in the imperial palace. Archaeologists excavated 11 pits and unearthed numerous cultural relics.

These two naked pottery figurines are very surprising. The major difference between them and the other naked pottery figurines is that they have no scrotums. This is not out of carelessness, but intention. They are the earliest images of eunuchs in China. To ensure the purity of the imperial blood, there should not be a second man in the imperial palace.

Besides the eunuchs, the emperor's daily life was mainly in the care of the maids of honor. They wore splendid clothes as well.

In people's imagination, the imperial life was rich and luxurious. However, the concept of wealth 2000 years ago was quite different from that of today.

The 92-meter-long No.13 attendant burial grave is the emperor's warehouse.

In a warehouse on the west side, there are two horses and chariots as big as the real objects. The painted wood horses and chariots are furnished with gold-plated bronze decorations. They are the luxurious chariots for the emperor's parade.

Farther west of it is a large warehouse of articles for daily use. A large number of painted pottery barns were unearthed. They are over 1 meter high, with some 30 barns in every row, and altogether there are more than 90 barns. The barns are filled with noodle-like food. In ancient times, food was the most precious of wealth. Common people were always worried about the shortage of food.

Of course the emperor didn't have to worry about this. He had not only abundant food to eat, but also a large amount of meat. In the No. 13 pit there were nearly 2,000 animal pottery figurines, including 231 painted pottery goats, 33 pottery lambs, 456 pottery dogs of various colors, some small pottery piglets, as well as roosters and hens.

Wang Baoping
Vice Curator of the Archaeological Museum of Yang Ling Mausoleum of Han

Just like a refrigerator at home, it's a buttery in the Han dynasty, with one layer of mutton, another of pork, and still another of dog meat. It was exquisite and beautiful. This represents the meat buttery in the imperial palace of Han during Emperor Jing's reign.

All the animals were vividly portrayed, with succinct strokes and smooth lines. Amidst the figurines there also stood waiters responsible for raising them.

People spent so much care in building such a symbolic imperial warehouse. What other treasures must have been hidden in those attendant burial graves unexposed?

The Pottery Eunuchs

The Emperor's Burial Objects

In order for people to appreciate the treasures in the Yang Ling Mausoleum, the Archaeological Museum of Yang Ling Mausoleum of Han was built and opened to the public in 1999. The exterior design of the museum is concise and modernistic, and its interior is full of originality as well.

Even in cold winters, there are many tourists that come here to visit.

The designer attempted to blend the style of the museum with that of the ancient relics. However, the spectacle of 2000 years ago cannot be completely restored even with the most advanced technology.

The mausoleum today appears a bit empty. Except the towering mounds, many places turned out to be wastelands or tillable fields. What was this place like in the 2nd century BC?

Through the many years of explorations and excavations, archaeologists finally made clear of the basic shape and structure of the Yang Ling Mausoleum. The mausoleum is in the shape of an irregular rectangle, which is 10 km from east to west and 1-3 km from north to south.

The emperor's and empress' mausoleums form, respectively, an enclosed courtyard. On

Animal Pottery Figurines

the four sides of the courtyards there were square ramparts. In the four directions of north, east, south and west in the ramparts, there is a gate named "Que Gateway."

Wang Baoping
Vice Curator of the Archaeological Museum of Yang Ling Mausoleum of Han

Que represents the overbearing royal ideas. According to history, whenever the prime minister went to the palace to report to the emperor, he had to stand outside the Que Gateway. This Que, has the same sound as Que, meaning defects. He had to stop here every time and reflect whether he had any defects. The function of the gateways in the ramparts is that people can live in the tops of them, and that they can also stand in a high place and guard the mausoleum.

Over the years, all the Que Gateways have been reduced to two hillocks. What were they like in the past?

The Archaeological Team carried out clearage and excavations on the sites of the Que Gateways in the south of the emperor's mausoleum. On the spot, they discovered many beam holes. There used to be huge wooden beams in the holes to support the tremendous construction. These pebbles in regular order are called "San Shui," the purpose of which is to prevent the rain from destroying the ground. They are placed right below the eaves. Archaeologists also cleaned up a few stairs, which indicate that the building was a high pavilion.

The remnant traces of charcoal indicates that there once was a big fire here, while the piles of broken tiles are proof of the building's collapse.

The greatest achievement of the clearage of the ruins is that many eaves' tiles were recovered. The eaves' tiles could protect the wooden rafters and decorate the building as well. These are the fluent cloud patterns similar to the fleeting clouds in the sky. There are also many eaves' tiles with characters, expressing such auspicious words as "Chang Le Wei Yang," "Qian Qiu Wan Sui," and such.

When all the sporadic archaeological proofs were pieced together, we arrived at a picture of the former Que Gateways.

Wang Baoping:

Some say what we see now is just a huge heap of earth. But actually, it was a platform base that the Han people built layer by layer 2143 years ago. The house on top was once grand and magnificent.

The Sand Table of Yang Ling Mausoleum

The Relic Site of the Southern Que Gateway

After the completion of the archaeological work, people constructed a restored large-scale building outside the site of the Southern Que Gateway in order to restore the former grandeur of the Han royalty.

"San Shui"

This Que Terrace is 131 meters wide from east to west, and 25.5 meters deep from north to south. On the roof of the terrace there were towering ridge gargoyles, and the roof was decorated with beautiful eaves tiles. The whole building was somber and elegant, much like the guards in the palace that protect the emperor's resting place.

At that time, emperors were the center of everyone's attention, and they would not be lonely after death. On the east of the Yang Ling Mausoleum there is the burial ground area, where high-ranking officials

Eaves' Tiles

A Restored Southern Que Gateway

The Emperor's Burial Objects

and eminent noblemen were buried. They surrounded the emperor at a proper distance, just as when they were alive. It was inferred that there were at least over 10,000 graves here. The archaeological team carried out excavations to some of the graves. Although a large part of the graves were damaged by tomb raiders, the remaining cultural relics provided us with a picture of the nobleman's life.

This large-scale underground group includes over 200 animal pottery figurines and over 200 human ones, as well as hundreds of articles of daily use. They were unearthed from an attendant burial grave of a nobleman. The identity of the host of the grave has not been made clear, but he must be a high-ranking minister.

Various potteries and bronze wares display all aspects of the ancients' daily life. Such things as ovens for cooking meals, containers of water and wine, as well as pottery barns for the storage of food, are all articles on which people depended in their lives. Naturally they wanted to bring them into the afterlife.

This bronze ware is a wine container. Perhaps the master once used it. Characters were inscribed on the bronze container, saying that this is the wine vessel of the Ban Yi family made in their No. 2 workshop, which could contain 10 dou of wine and weighed 17.5 kg.

The Animal Pottery Figurines in the Eastern Attendant Burial Graves

This is an ancient cooking utensil. The lower pot can contain water and the upper part food. When heated, it can steam the food. Its master was perhaps an eminent duke or princess.

These decorations on the weapons are also made of bronze. Despite their small sizes, they were exquisite in workmanship and very stylized. They are also precious works of art.

The luxuriant life of the noblemen is always accompanied with a lot of servants.

Ancient Cooking Utensils

The Bronze Decorations on the Weapons

He is a retainer in charge of daily domestic affairs. His airs are scrupulous, his clothes clean and orderly, and his obedient face the embodiment of humility.

The maids are also meek in expression, but their postures are much more lively.

She is waiting for her master to call. She is absorbed in playing the fiddle. She is waving her long sleeves and dancing happily.

These girls are low in position. Most of them are maids or musicians. But the craftsmen endowed them with the most beautiful faces.

They have slim bodies, long and fine brows, big eyes, and chubby faces. Their long black hair was coiled in the back of their heads and combed into buns at the bottom.

The colorful paintings finely and faithfully represented their attires. Almost no girls wore jewelry. The long loose skirts were contracted at their waists and spread bell-like at the bottom, which properly drew the outline of their slim female bodies. The garments were not luxuriant, with some decorations at the necklines and sleeves.

Wang Xueli
Research fellow of the Shaanxi Archaeological Institute

This had a name in the Han dynasty, that is, Pian Zhu Yuan. So when women pottery figurines wore these dresses, their long skirts hung over the ground. When they stood or walked, they looked very elegant and graceful. This reflects that the upper-class women in the royal court of Han were very particular about their clothes. They had a taste for beauty.

All these have provided us with ancient life scenes.

With the gradual development of the archaeological work, more became known about the past and the ancestors' thoughts became gradually understood.

In ancient China, imperial mausoleums were the symbol of the uppermost royal power. Everything should be arranged and furnished according to the rituals in the emperor's lifetime. The spectacle of the former imperial palace was completely laid out in the Yang Ling Mausoleum, which covers an area of a dozen square km.

On the north of the emperor's mausoleum

The Emperor's Burial Objects

there is an especially conspicuous burial grave. Its hostess was Concubine Li, the favorite concubine of Emperor Jing. The emperor had entitled her son as the royal prince, and even prepared to confer the empress title on her.

However, it was not long before another woman turned up. She is the other master of the Yang Ling Mausoleum, Empress Wang.

Empress Wang was of low origin. She had married a low-ranking nobleman and gave birth to a daughter. When her mother knew that the emperor would select beauties, she asked her daughter to desert her husband and child and to go to the palace as a maid of honor.

The Maid with the Beautiful Face   The Maid Dancing

A Figurine Retainer in Charge of Daily Domestic Affairs   The Maid Playing the Fiddle   The Maid Waiting for Her Master to Call

215

Paving Bricks

"Luo Jing Stone"

The beautiful and sly girl finally won the emperor's trust through many struggles. She became the empress, her son the royal prince, whereas Concubine Li lost the emperor's favor and died in loneliness and pain.

In any period, women are always the indispensable heroines of the stories. However, what we can see today are only moss-grown tombs.

Before the Archaeological Team came to the Yang Ling Mausoleum, the local folk had their own ideas and guessed about the graves. On the southeast of the emperor's mausoleum, there was a strange stone. The local people called it "Luo Jing Stone," meaning a compass-like stone. It is the highest point of the whole mausoleum area, as the "Luo Jing Stone" is over 5 meters higher than the surrounding ground. What is the use of this stone? Why is it placed in such a conspicuous place?

Before the archaeological excavation, people once thought that the stone was used for standardizing levels, measuring height, and marking directions. However, the result of the tentative explorations in 1998 gave rise to doubts over this opinion.

The archaeologists have basically confirmed that this is a site of a square building, with moats surrounding the outer sides. In the center of the moats there were 4 majestic gates.

The large amount of unearthed bricks and tiles has testified to the result of the explorations. Some bricks for paving the ground have been preserved intact, on the surface of which were inscribed beautiful patterns. The patterns were joined together into fluent and regular lines, which is very much like today's luxuriant paving bricks. Among the large number of eaves tiles, people also discovered a 1-meter-long huge pantile, which indicates that the building used to be very grand and majestic. Its scale was far greater than that of the Southern Que Gateway and the building might be used for ritual sacrifices.

Such evidence has deepened the doubts about the "Luo Jing Stone." Was it indeed used for the determination of directions? If not, what was it for?

Wang Baoping
Vice Curator of the Archaeological Museum of Yang Ling Mausoleum of Han

The excavated archaeological documents showed that it wasn't the so-called "Luo Jing Stone" at all. It was only the central beam of this central building. According to the present array of the round beam holes, there should have been 169 round beams. The building was a very large temple or palace. It covered an area of 103 mu and the scale is enormous. The area as confined by this group of holes is thousands of square meters. Such a site of ritual buildings is the first discovery in all the mausoleums in China.

The archaeological excavations of the site of "Luo Jing Stone" are still under way.

More than 2000 years ago, people spent 28 years building the Yang Ling Mausoleum, whereas today, a dozen years of archaeological excavations has only revealed a small part of it. How much time in the future shall we wait to have a complete look into the emperor's underground palace?

Mysteries of Statues of Buddha in Qingzhou

They were one of the most exciting archaeological discoveries in China in the 20th century. The more than 400 exquisite statues of Buddha were sculptured between the 5th and 6th centuries. They had been buried underground and lying in the darkness for a thousand years.

They waked up after a long sleep, disclosing secrets from the remote past.

Mysteries of Statues of Buddha in Qingzhou

In the autumn of 2001, Berlin, Germany was in a warm atmosphere of the Asia-Pacific Culture and Art Festival.

Preparatory work was underway for a component of the festival. It was the Exhibition of Statues of Buddha from Qingzhou, China.

Unearthed five years earlier, these statues were on display abroad for the first time. The 33 items were only a small part of the cultural relics unearthed in Qingzhou, but the visitors were very much impressed by the splendid exhibition.

These exquisite statues came from Qingzhou, Shandong Province, China. For German visitors who had learned about Chinese history, it was a faraway but not unfamiliar place.

At the end of the 19th century, Western colonialists flooded into China. German troops occupied a port along the coast of Shandong Province and built a railway from the port to the hinterland. Qingzhou was a small station along the railway.

Built a hundred years ago, the railway is one of the busiest transport lines in China today. In summer every year, many people from the hinterland travel along this railway to holiday resorts along the coast. Only slow trains stop at Qingzhou for a few minutes. Without the astonishing discovery in the autumn of 1996, Qingzhou probably would have remained a small city that could not attract the attention of passengers going to holiday resorts.

One day in October, 1996, construction of a sports ground was in full swing at a school in Qingzhou. The driver of a bulldozer found something unusual. Workers pushed aside the earth in front of the bulldozer. They were astonished by what they saw. The hoard of statues of

Mysteries of Statues of Buddha in Qingzhou

Buddha was discovered by chance.

The Museum of Qingzhou City stands at the centre of the city. When you look down from the top floor of the museum, you will find that the statues of Buddha were unearthed just beyond the wall close to the museum.

Xia Mingcai, then a deputy curator of Qingzhou Museum, inspected the hoard of statues.

Xia Mingcai

Former Deputy Curator of Museum of Qingzhou City
  Here was the hoard. It was 8.6 metres long from west to east and 6.7 metres wide from north to south. Here was the east edge.

Rescue archaeological excavation of the statues of Buddha began promptly.

The Archaeological Excavation Scene of the Statues of Buddha in Longxing Temple

The Triple Images of Buddha in the Late Northern Wei Dynasty

Archaeologists worked for seven days and nights. The statues covered with earth gradually showed their original features.

Sun Xinsheng

Former Deputy Curator of Museum of Qingzhou City
  A big stone was covered with earth. We couldn't see the true features. After we washed away the earth, the statues looked very fresh.

221

Xia Mingcai
Former Deputy Curator of Museum of Qingzhou City

A complete statue of the Goddess of Mercy was lying there when it was unearthed. It was quite graceful. People said Venus was beautiful. It seemed to me that the statues here were more beautiful than Venus.

It was probably the most exciting moment. It displayed the most fantastic splendour of archaeology. When beautiful faces emerged from the earth one after another, everybody asked: Who were they? Where did they come from?

Mysteries arose when the archaeological excavation began. First of all, people wondered why so many statues of Buddha had been buried at such a small place.

It seemed to be easy to answer this question. Before the hoard was discovered, local people learned that a temple had existed here in ancient times. According to the county annals, it was called Longxing Temple. Around A.D. 500, it was a large temple known far and wide. It attracted a great many worshippers for more than 800 years. Strangely the temple disappeared around A.D. 1300.

Today people can only imagine the history of Longxing Temple from a stone tablet unearthed from the ruins of the temple. What was the relationship between the statues of Buddha unearthed from the

The Goddess of Mercy Lying in the Site of Archaeological Excavation

Mysteries of Statues of Buddha in Qingzhou

ruins of the temple and the temple itself?

More questions came up with the progress of archaeological excavation. After the broken pieces were fitted together and restored, the number of statues exceeded 400. Why had so many statues of Buddha been buried in a pit with a space of only over 50 square metres and a depth of less than three metres? Many statues could not be restored to their original forms. They were merely incomplete parts or heads of statues. Some fragments showed that they had been smashed. Who had smashed them? Why had they been smashed? Why had these statues been buried carefully? What secrets were hidden behind the broken pieces and restored statues?

The discovery at Qingzhou caused a sensation in the archaeological circles in Beijing. The State Cultural Relics Bureau promptly organized a group of experts for an appraisal in Qingzhou.

Located on the Shandong Peninsula, Qingzhou was one of the nine administrative divisions of ancient China. Its historical origin dates back 7,000 years. Many historical remains verify the brilliance of this city in the past.

What historical secrets would the unearthed statues of Buddha disclose?

The appraisal was not a difficult job. From the carving skills and motifs the

The Colored Image of Bodhisattva

archaeologists found that most of the statues were sculptured between the 5th and 6th centuries. In those days, the world was in a period of great turmoil.

At the middle of the first millennium after the birth of Jesus Christ, similar events took place in Europe and China almost simultaneously. The Roman Empire was heading for extinction under the pressure of ethnic groups from the north. At the same time, the Jin Dynasty in China, a reign of the Han people, was disintegrating under the impact of ethnic groups from the northern grasslands. Aristocrats in exile continued the reign of the Han rulers in the south. Different regimes of ethnic groups from the grasslands came into being in the north. In A.D. 439, the Xianbei (鲜卑) ethnic group from the Greater Hinggan Mountains established the Northern Wei (魏)Dynasty and unified the north. Then in the north emerged the Eastern Wei, Western Wei, Northern Qi (齐)and Northern Zhou (周)dynasties. The more than 200 years were a period of the worst turmoil in Chinese history. It was known as the Northern and Southern Dynasties.

Most of the statues of Buddha in Qingzhou were sculptured in that period.

The oldest statues date back to the late Northern Wei Dynasty. They are not many in number. Most of them have back screens. This was one of the forms of statues introduced from Central Asia.

Most of them are triple images of Buddha. On each side of such a set is an image of Bodhisattva. At the centre is the image of Sakyamuni, founder of Buddhism.

Sakyamuni was the prince of a kingdom in ancient India. He gave up his position and wealth, left his parents and wife, and went to the remote mountains and wilderness to seek vimukta (or deliverance) and the true meaning of life. At last he attained bodhi (or awakening) and founded Buddhism. Sakyamuni experienced and transcended sufferings all his life. The smiling face of the statue of the Buddhist patriarch reveals the joy in his innermost being. This is a peculiar Chinese explanation of Buddhism.

The pedestals beneath the statues of Buddha and Bodhisattva bear carvings of lotus flowers. The legend goes that when Sakyamuni founded Buddhism under a bodhi tree, a pair of lotus flowers bloomed at his side. The lotus flower became an auspicious pattern of Buddhism. The image of the dragon, a totem in ancient China, was also visible at the pedestal of the statue of Buddha. This had never been seen from statues of Buddha unearthed in other parts of China.

Jin Weinuo

Professor of Central Academy of Fine Arts

Buddhism was popular in Southern Yan during the Period of Sixteen States.People believed in auspicious signs. So temples were named after the dragon. The flying dragon appeared as an auspicious sign in Qingzhou. There were not so many temples named after the dragon in other areas. The dragon pattern was characteristic of statues of Buddha in Qingzhou.

Mysteries of Statues of Buddha in Qingzhou

The Triple Images of Buddha with Back Screen

A dragon pillar was unearthed from the ruins of Longxing Temple. The coiling dragon on the pillar and the flying dragon on the statue spitting lotus flowers remind people of Longxing Temple, because Longxing literally means a rising dragon. The gorgeously carved dragons created a dynamic world in the remote past.

The back screens behind the statues of Buddha sculptured during the Northern Wei and Eastern Wei dynasties were made to show Buddha's halo. This was an important mark to differentiate the Buddhist deities from human beings. Images of the flying Apsaras were delicately carved in relief on the upper parts of many back screens. The beautiful angels seemed to be floating up to the legendary paradise in Buddhism. They had subtle ties with the flying Apsaras portrayed on murals in Dunhuang Grottoes. To reach the other world of utmost happiness, one had to go through the most miserable trials and tribulations. The coloured drawing of raging flames under the flying Apsaras signified the process of suffering. The Northern and Southern Dynasties were a period of great turmoil full of conspiracies, betrayals and massacres. Almost nobody and no region could escape the turmoil. In those years, religion displayed the power that had never been seen before.

Around the first century, Buddhism was introduced into China by merchants and monks from Central Asia, but Buddhism had little influence in those days. After the 4th century, Buddhism developed in China at a much faster pace with the collapse of the dynasty of the Han people and the shaking of the authoritative status of Confucianism.

After the Northern Wei Dynasty was established, Buddhism was gradually combined with politics. The emperors, empresses and aristocrats of the imperial family were pious believers and promoters of Buddhism. Construction of grottoes with huge statues of Buddha began on a large scale. It was said that the statues were modeled after the emperors.

Buddhism became a Noah's ark for people to free themselves from wars and sufferings. Statues of Buddha were sculptured in many parts of the country.

Images of the Flying Apsaras Delicately Carved in Relief on the Back Screen

Mysteries of Statues of Buddha in Qingzhou

It was a period of great enthusiasm for religious belief and a period of mass creation of idols.

Many statues of Buddha were also sculptured in Qingzhou, a link between the Northern Dynasties and the Southern Dynasties. Situated in the central region politically and culturally, Qingzhou became a place where many grottoes and statues of Buddhism were built. In the vicinity of Qingzhou today, we still can see some Buddhist grottoes built between the 6th and 7th centuries.

While these grottoes were constructed, many temples were built and images of Buddha and Bodhisattva were enshrined in the temples. From the stone tablet unearthed at the ruins of Longxing Temple, we can presume that the temple was called Nanyang Temple. As the most prominent temple in the area, it boasted a towering pagoda and a magnificent hall. A huge statue of Buddha with a height of 13 metres stands at the centre of the hall.

No huge statues of Buddha were found from those unearthed at the ruins of Longxing Temple, but some of them are three metres high, not including the height of their pedestals. Their carving skills were so admirable that people wondered who sculptured the statues and how they felt when they did the job.

Xia Mingcai
Former Deputy Curator of Museum of Qingzhou City

I believe some monks of Longxing Temple specialized in this profession. In lamaseries in Tibet today, there are craftsmen making coloured butter figurines or painting Tangkars. I think such a situation existed at Longxing Temple in those days. When they sculptured statues with chisels, they displayed their reverence and worship for Buddha and Bodhisattva.

Of course, this is only a reasonable presumption. We can hardly verify the true creators of these statues of Buddha.

The Buddhist Grotto Built between the 6th and 7th Centuries in Qingzhou

The Present Stone Carvers in Qingzhou Making Sculptures Out of Limestone

But it is certain that the carving skills in Qingzhou attained a fairly high level.

Most of the statues of Buddha in Qingzhou were carved out of limestone. Fine and appropriately hard, the limestone is particularly fit for sculpturing exquisite statues. Making sculptures out of limestone is a tradition which still survives today. Many craftsmen are from families of stone carvers. Are they descendants of those who sculptured the statues of Buddha in Qingzhou?

This is a statue of a man of a northern tribe of the Eastern Han Dynasty unearthed in the area. It is preserved at the Museum of Qingzhou City. Carved roughly but vividly, the statue is three metres high. This proves that large statues could already be carved delicately in those days. Over 300 years later, the local stone carvers devoted their excellent skills to the belief in Buddhism.

Before the hoard at Longxing Temple was discovered, some other statues of Buddha had been unearthed in Qingzhou and the adjacent areas. The total number exceeded 1,000. These statues and those of Longxing Temple were made almost in the same period. They confirm that Qingzhou was not only a centre of Buddhism, but also a centre for the sculpture of statues of Buddha.

The Head of Buddha Sculptured between the Late Northern Wei Dynasty and the Eastern Wei Dynasty

Like what occurred in the history of civilization in many other parts of the world, the close ties between art and religion have been verified in Qingzhou again. When the wisdom of human beings and their devout religious belief were combined, immense enthusiasm for creation was kindled.

After Buddhism was introduced into China from India, the Chinese began to make idols. The early statues of Buddha showed influence from Central Asia and India. The mixture of different cultures brought forth statues of Buddha with Chinese features.

A Statue of a Man of a Northern Tribe of the Eastern Han Dynasty Unearthed in the Area

The Statue of Buddha Wearing the Loose Robe with a Broad Waistband

The Round Sculpture of Buddha during the Northern Qi Dynasty

Most of the statues of Buddha sculptured in Qingzhou between the late Northern Wei Dynasty and the Eastern Wei Dynasty were marked by thin figures and drooping shoulders. They were typical of the Han people in China.

The cheekbones of the statues were slightly prominent. They were images of wise men in traditional Chinese culture. The well-chiselled features of statues showed much influence from the traditional aesthetic tastes of the literati of the Han people. Such a style was first popular in the south dominated by Han rulers and promptly spread to the north.

The style of garments carved on statues of Buddha also showed influence from the south dominated by Han rulers. After Buddha came to China from India, its statue wore the loose robe with a broad waistband. This was typical of the traditional garment of the Han people.

The Han style of statues of Buddha was an epitome of the Han inclination of the dynasties established by ethnic groups on the northern grasslands.

The war turmoil and breakup didn't obstruct cultural interflow during the Northern and Southern Dynasties. The grassland ethnic groups that controlled the north began to learn the culture of the Han people from the dynasties in the south. The Han inclination was most dynamic during the reign of Emperor Xiaowen of Northern Wei.

They followed the dress style, etiquette and institutions of the Southern Dynasties. It was something like a cultural revival for those Han people living in the north.

Mysteries of Statues of Buddha in Qingzhou

Qingzhou was a hub of transportation between the north and the south. It was once under the jurisdiction of the Southern Dynasties. The culture of the north and that of the south were mixed here for a long time. Naturally cultural influence from the dynasties of the Han people in the south was manifested in the sculpture of statues of Buddha. The shapes of statues were close to the physical shapes of the Han people. The traditional Chinese long gown was portrayed. Such a graceful style lasted until Eastern Wei in the first half of the 6th century.

But when we observe the statues of Buddha sculptured during Northern Qi in the 6th century, we find that the well-chiselled features of statues were replaced by a new style. Relief sculptures with back screens almost disappeared. Most of the round sculptures showed plump faces. As compared with the thick garments carved on statues during Northern Wei, the statues made during Northern Qi displayed utterly different aesthetic tastes.

The thin and nicely-fit clothes of all the statues revealed healthy and graceful figures. The artistic style introduced from India in the early days became the main style once again. It took only a hundred years for the Chinese-style statues wearing loose robes with broad waistbands during the Northern Wei and Eastern Wei dynasties to evolve into the alien-style statues made during the Northern Qi Dynasty. What caused the drastic change? Why did the old style disappear completely?

Zhang Zong

Research Fellow of Chinese Academy of Social Sciences

It certainly proved cultural exchange in those days. In the history of Chinese culture, there were many tribes in the north during the Northern Dynasties. The Tuoba tribe of the Xianbei ethnic group learned and assimilated the Han culture. Their statues of Buddha were Sinicized. During the late Northern Dynasties, the ruler Gao Huan was a Han man. But he had learned Xianbei culture. He grew up at Liuzheng in the north. When he was a child, he was influenced by Xianbei folkways. So folkways of northern tribes prevailed during the Northern Qi Dynasty. The area had a lot of contact with Xinjiang. This was probably the cultural background of the Indian-style statues of Buddha.

The rubbing from a stone carving of the Northern Qi Dynasty unearthed in Qingzhou proved that people of northern tribes were engaged in economic and cultural activities widely in

The Head of Buddha Sculpured in the Northern Qi Dynasty

231

Qingzhou. The exchanges were also displayed in the sculpture of statues of Buddha.

Some statues presented images of people of northern tribes in low relief or coloured drawing.

Some statues showed lines of garments carved in anaglyph. They looked like wet clothes clinging to the bodies. Some other statues showed no wrinkles. Their outlines fully displayed the beauty of human bodies. Such statues were quite rare in the north and on the Central Plains in those days. This was probably the wet-clothing drawing mentioned in historical records, a style of painting in which clothing appeared to be wet, clinging to the human body.

Zhang Zong
Research Fellow of Chinese Academy of Social Sciences

Cao Zhongda was a master painter during the Northern Qi Dynasty. In fact, he was a Sogdian. He came from Central Asia to do business. He belonged to the branch with the surname "Cao". He painted the image of Buddha in the Cao style of wet-clothing drawing. It was typical of the image of Buddha in an Indian style.

Circles of close lines were very clear on the statues of Buddha in Qingzhou carved during the Northern Qi Dynasty. Some statues of Buddha were sculptured in the style of Mrgadava. Their bodies are apparent almost without wrinkles of clothing. Only a few wrinkles can be seen on the cuffs of sleeves. This pattern is also obvious on the statues of Buddha in Qingzhou.

The Standing Statue of the Goddess of Mercy Sculptured during the Northern Qi Dynasty

Why was the genre of wet-clothing drawing introduced from the Western Regions thousands of kilometres away from Qingzhou? Even today, opinions are quite divided on this question, because similar statues have not been found in other areas. Did they come along the Silk Road? Did Cao Jiaxiang enter southern China from Vietnam and then come to Qingzhou along a water route as many historians presumed?

Anyhow it is certain that after the new style was introduced into Qingzhou, the local craftsmen mixed it with their own skills. Statues of Buddha with new features were sculptured during the Northern Qi Dynasty.

The statues of Buddha sculptured during the Northern Qi Dynasty showed simple and lively features, but the statues of Bodhisattva sculptured during the same period presented a style of complexity, nicety and magnificence.

Here we see the luxurious headgear, the exquisite neckband, the fluttering cloak and the fine objects attached to the cloak. These ornaments were delicately carved.

These statues of Bodhisattva with gorgeous ornaments were decorated with coloured drawings and covered with gold foil. We can imagine the resplendence of the statues in those days.

The Standing Statue of the Goddess of Mercy (from the back)

The standing statue of the Goddess of Mercy was a unique masterpiece of Buddhist art. The calm and composed face conveys the solemnity and tranquility of the dharma-realm. It seems that we can feel what she is thinking about and what she wants to express. But all returns to eternal silence.

The statue of Bodhisattva of Thought is a special one. It portrays Sakyamuni meditating under a bodhi tree and attaining bodhi at last. The elegant posture, the incomplete gilded parts with coloured drawings and the damaged left arm arouse fanciful thoughts. The mysterious smile on the baby-like face seems to reveal the fact that he has realized the true meaning of Buddhism through meditation.

Everybody who has seen the statues of Buddha in Qingzhou is filled with great admiration for the wonderful carving skills and superb achievements of art. He is eager to know more about these statues.

From the county annals we can presume that as a centre of Buddhism in those days, Qingzhou attracted devout believers from all directions. They burned joss sticks before images of Buddha, praying for Buddha's blessing in the turbulent days. People donated a lot of money to the sculpture of statues of Buddha.

Among the statues unearthed from the ruins of Longxing Temple, the statue

The Statue of Bodhisattva of Thought during the Northern Qi Dynasty

Mysteries of Statues of Buddha in Qingzhou

The Sculpture of the Statue Donated by a Lady Named Han Xiaohua

sculptured during Northern Wei was carved with the donator's inscription.

This was a lady by the name of Han Xiaohua. It seemed that she lived alone. In the inscription she listed the names of her deceased husband and close relatives. She hoped that the deities would remember their names and ensured that they would enjoy peace, riches and honour and remain devout to Buddha in their next transmigration. Judging from the size and carving of the statue, we presume that Han Xiaohua was probably not a wealthy lady and perhaps she donated all her savings to the sculpture of this statue.

Through the inscriptions on the statues, we can get more information related to them. Only a few statues with such inscriptions have been unearthed in Qingzhou. We find that such an inscription was carved on the side of a statue or at the bottom of a statue. In ancient times, a pedestal was made while a statue was sculptured. Information on the very statue was carved on the pedestal. But no pedestals with inscriptions were found from the statues of Buddha unearthed at the ruins of Longxing Temple in Qingzhou.

Ma Shichang

Professor of Peking University

We found it had a tenon, but we didn't find the pedestal. In other words, we didn't find pedestals with vows-taking inscriptions. So we think when more excavation was done at the ruins of Longxing Temple, stone statue pedestals with vows-taking inscriptions will possibly be discovered.

But no more statue pedestals were found from the continuing excavation. Where had they gone? This question reminded us of a greater mystery, namely the burial of statues of Buddha at Longxing Temple. Why hadn't the pedestals and the statues been buried together? Why had the statues been buried?

After the statues of Buddha in Qingzhou were unearthed, the archaeologists were puzzled by the question why so many exquisite statues of Buddha had been buried underground. They found that the

Chinese Archaeological Discoveries

The Slope at the Middle of the Pit

statues had been smashed before burial. Why had the statues been smashed? Had the same group of people smashed and buried the statues?

A slope at the middle of the pit led to the bottom of the pit. It should have been designed for the diggers to carry and store the statues.

Most of the statues in the pit were severely damaged, but three layers of broken pieces were arranged in good order. The fairly complete statues were put at the middle layer. The archaeologists found veins of reed mats on the top layer of statues. They prove that the statues were covered with reed mats before burial.

All the details prove that the burial was well planned. Those who took part in the burial were most probably devout believers in Buddhism. Why did they have no alternative but to bury the statues? Who smashed the statues?

Jin Weinuo
Professor of Central Academy of Fine Arts

We guess that it had something to do with the suppression of Buddhism. Two suppressions of Buddhism took place in the late Tang Dynasty and Five Dynasties. The stone statues were probably damaged after the suppressions of Buddhism.

Traces of burning and restoration are visible from some statues. Probably they were damaged in the suppressions of Buddhism during the Northern and Southern Dynasties and restored with the revival of Buddhism in the later period.

New clues to the time of burial emerged with the progress of archaeological work.

Some statues found from the pit at Longxing Temple were judged to have been sculptured during the Northern Song Dynasty. One statue bears characters meaning "the fourth year of the Tiansheng period of the Northern Song", namely A.D. 1026. It was almost 500 years after the last suppression of Buddhism during the Northern and Southern Dynasties. This reversed the conclusion that the statues of Buddha were destroyed in the suppression of Buddhism during the Northern and Song Dynasties and buried later. There were no records of suppression of Buddhism in the history of Northern Song. Did a more terrible disaster occur during Northern Song, causing the damage and burial of the statues of Buddha?

Mysteries of Statues of Buddha in Qingzhou

The Sculpture of Statue Made during the Northern Song Dynasty

Xia Mingcai
Former Deputy Curator of Museum of Qingzhou City

A great turmoil occurred in China at the end of Northern Song. With the invasion of Jin troops, Emperor Huizong and Emperor Qinzong were captured and escorted to the north. Longxing Temple stood south of the west gate of Nanyang, Qingzhou. It was close to the city wall. According to historical records, Jin troops attacked Qingzhou five times in three years. They stormed into the city five times and withdrew four times. Fierce battles were fought near Longxing Temple. I believe statues of Buddha at Longxing Temple were destroyed in those battles.

According to Xia Mingcai's presumption, monks of Longxing Temple dug the pit, carefully carried the statues along this slope and piled up three layers of statues and broken pieces. The traces of burning on statues were caused by burning paper and joss sticks.

Xia Mingcai:

We are studying a clay sculpture. There are some disputes. It is a pottery basin about 30 centimetres in diameter. It was a common basin for daily use. If it had been a dry clay sculpture, the basin would have been unnecessary. The clay sculpture was flattened. It can be identified barely as an image of Buddha. The clay sculpture was made of a monk's ashes. It happened that a monk at Longxing Temple died. His ashes were used to make the image guarding the statues of Buddha.

Were the statues of Buddha in Qingzhou

The Statues of Buddha in Qingzhou

destroyed during the southward invasion of Jin troops? People questioned this presumption from different angles.

Ma Shichang
Professor of Peking University

If that was true, statues of Buddha destroyed at the time of the southward invasion of Jin troops should have been found elsewhere. But we haven't found examples in other areas. We have found many vows-taking inscriptions of Jin Dynasty in northern Shaanxi. It proves that people had Buddhist activities in those days. Buddhist believers sculptured statues in grottoes. It proves that no serious damage was caused to Buddhism during Jin Dynasty.

If the statues of Buddha had not been buried during the suppression of Buddhism of the Northern and Southern Dynasties or during the southward invasion of Jin troops, what caused them to sleep in the earth for such a long time?

Archaeologists turned their attention to a stone tablet unearthed near Qingzhou. The inscription on the stone tablet might be the key to the mystery of the statues of Buddha in Qingzhou.

Yang Hong

Research Fellow of Chinese Academy of Social Sciences

Many ancient statues of Buddha were found in Linqu County in the early 1980s. They were similar to statues in Qingzhou. An inscription on the sculpture of statues was also unearthed. It referred to Mingdao Temple. Monks at the temple saw incomplete statues of Buddha. They brought them together and buried them. They also built a stupa on the burial site. Local officials and monks from nearby temples attended the grand service. After the service, a stone tablet with an inscription was buried there.

According to the inscription on the stone tablet, Master Yiyong, abbot of Longxing Temple, attended the service on a day in the first year of the Jingde period, namely A.D.1004. This date was identical to the time when the hoarding took place at Longxing Temple. From this clue we can presume that during the Northern Song Dynasty, Buddhist services prevailed at temples in Qingzhou. Monks collected statues of Buddha damaged in the suppressions of Buddhism and those worn out over the years. Then they held a solemn ceremony to bury the broken statues in

Mysteries of Statues of Buddha in Qingzhou

The Head of Buddha Sculptured during the Northern Qi Dynasty

order to accumulate merits. This can explain why many of the hoarded statues belonged to the Northern and Southern Dynasties when suppressions of Buddhism occurred and only a few statues date back to the Sui, Tang and Northern Song dynasties.

But people are still puzzled by one mystery. If the statues of Buddha were buried during the Northern Song Dynasty, the gold foil and coloured drawings on the statues should have faded away over the centuries. But even today, the statues sculptured about a thousand years ago still display fantastic lustre and brilliant colour. How should this be explained?

Ma Shichang
Professor of Peking University

So I doubt that these statues were buried a long time ago. Especially statues of Northern Dynasties were probably buried in the suppression of Buddhism during Northern Song. A few statues were mixed with them later. They were put into the hoard.

There is another explanation for why the statues of Buddha in Qingzhou retain their brilliant colour. From many pedestals, archaeologists found the character meaning "gold" written in Chinese ink. It was a mark for Buddhist believers to apply gilding and colour drawing on the old statues once again.

But this presumption is not reasonable if we refer to the way the statues were buried. If statues were already damaged, it was unnecessary to restore them before they were buried. Why has the brilliant colour remained till today?

Every seemingly correct answer is shadowed by many possibilities and presumptions. The final answers to the puzzles related to the statues in Qingzhou have not been found yet. When we gaze at the beautiful facial features dating back a thousand years, perhaps the answers are no longer important. Their secrets were sealed up with the mysterious burial many centuries ago, but these great works of art are displaying their fantastic luster again. This is a most exciting miracle.

撰　　稿：张东霞　许　蕾　高　原　徐海婴
　　　　　赵平洋　刘湘晨　刘　洋　李东才
　　　　　刘　苏　卫　明

图片提供：孙良刚　赵　阳　刘湘晨　张鹿行
　　　　　徐海婴　吉　刚　赵平洋　高　原
　　　　　毕鲁克　赵伟东　陈道一　张梓羲
　　　　　叶　晶　赵永卫

图书在版编目（CIP）数据

马王堆传奇/张东霞，许蕾等著；张克士译.
—北京：五洲传播出版社，2007.1
（考古中国）
ISBN 7-5085-1047-X

Ⅰ.马... Ⅱ.①张... ②许... ③张... Ⅲ.马王堆汉墓—考古发现—普及读物—英文 Ⅳ.K878.84-49

中国版本图书馆CIP数据核字（2006）第145446号

总 策 划：李 冰
策　　划：郭长建　李向平
主　 编：张东霞
副 主 编：孙良刚　许 蕾

策划编辑：荆孝敏
责任编辑：张美景　荆孝敏
编　 辑：龙力莉　王 昕　胡旭华　王 睿
图片编辑：闫志杰　刘 鹏　刘 娜
设计总监：闫志杰
设计制作：刘 鹏　刘 娜

马王堆传奇

五洲传播出版社
地址：北京市海淀区北小马厂6号华天大厦24层
邮编：100038
电话：(8610) 58891280/58880274
网址：www.cicc.org.cn

开本：170mm×227mm　1/16
字数：210千字
印张：15
版次：2007年1月第1版第1次印刷
印刷：北京画中画印刷有限公司
印数：1-2000册
书号：ISBN 7-5085-1047-X/K·792

定价：140.00元